50 Leadership Keys That Work

First Edition, September 2012
Printed in the United States of America

Other Books and Leadership materials may be ordered through booksellers or by contacting:

City Limits International
P.O. Box 6086
Elgin, Illinois, 60121
www.coaching4ministers.com

50 Leadership Keys That Work

Dr. David P. Robinson, PhD
www.coaching4ministers.com

City Limits International

Dedication

Along with my wife Marie and our wonderful family of three children, nine grandchildren and a great-grandson, I dedicate this book to those who have had a great impact on our efforts to extend God's Kingdom both in the Church world and the Marketplace. They include my parents, my brothers and sisters and extended family. They include those I have served in the church and business leaders in the marketplace. They were patient and taught me so much. It would take pages to list everyone. I owe them a debt I could never pay. As someone so aptly said, "If we see further down the road today it's because we stand on the shoulders of those who have gone before us."

Forward

'Everything in life rises and falls on Leadership!'

This short but simple statement is so very true and yet so overlooked that it hardly is known today. Leadership is the key to living a powerful, successful, and rewarding life... why don't more people recognize this?

Life can be lived in a reactive mode, where we react to situations and look to solve problems as they occur. In fact, almost all life is lived in this fashion and most of our educational systems operate this way. As a result, a majority of people live their lives in this fashion, reacting and managing things as they occur.

On the other hand, life can be lived in a proactive mode where individuals look at creating solutions before problems arise and anticipate steps to be taken to better position themselves and their affairs. Being proactive challenges people to think, it causes them to anticipate and consider what may occur, and it requires both insight and evaluation. In other words, being proactive requires an understanding and application of leadership principles.

Leadership is the key!

David and I have talked at length about one of our greatest needs in the world today – real, genuine leadership! Somehow we have concluded that leaders are born (i.e. – 'He's a born leader!'). Alternately, we've developed the thought that we have one leader and everyone else is a follower. The problem with these conclusions is the fact that we can automatically disqualify ourselves from becoming leaders and/or learning these leadership principles. Everyone in the world needs to realize their leadership potential – as individuals, parents, business owners, community volunteers, church leaders, etc.

Leadership is the key!

David Robinson is a veteran leader, a man of many dimensions, and vastly qualified to bring these principles to our attention. David has been sharing these principles by email for several years and has now brought all of these powerful principles together in this book for our understanding and edification.

Over the years of my professional practice as an attorney and businessman as well as my 25+ years of ministry and speaking, I have seldom met individuals who have the knowledge, wisdom, and experience that David brings to the table. As you begin reading this book, please keep this thought in mind – you're looking into the experiences and wisdom of a man who has studied, tested, and proven these principles in real life over 46 years and counting! And not just in one environment or discipline, David has proven these principles in pastoral ministry, the business world, the financial world, and all over the world as a mentor, coach, and encourager of people and leaders worldwide! That's what leadership is all about!

Remember, Leadership is the key!

Your life will be strengthened and expanded by the principles contained herein. Make the decision to read the entire book thoroughly and ready yourself for transformation. Then I would suggest you commit to reading, studying, and implementing the truths in a chapter per week! You will be amazed at the impact these principles will have on your life!

I want to personally thank you David for summarizing these valuable principles in this book for all to read and apply. You've impacted my life and brought me to a higher level, and for that, I am very grateful!

Dr Brian D Scott
HBA, LLB, D. Min
Victory Christian Centre &
Wealth Producers Ministry
London, Ontario

Contents

Endorsements

What's the difference between knowledge and wisdom? I believe knowledge is knowing WHAT to do, and wisdom is knowing HOW to do it. David Robinson and this book are a gift to every leader. David brings concrete wisdom to leaders on the frontline of business, academia and politics. What I would have paid to have this book in my hands when I was starting as a leader!

—Don Riling, Founder & CEO Riling Leadership Resources

This book will elevate your effectiveness as a leader—especially in those difficult and challenging situations. The practical insight and wisdom from Coach David is priceless and will give you a step-by-step process to lead your team to greater fruitfulness for the Kingdom!

Ray and Christy Wilkerson
Maoz Israel Ministries—Dallas, TX

In his latest book, David Robinson presents his acute understanding of management and team building dynamics. He captures the essential leadership tools in a way that will enhance the study and teaching of these critical principles necessary to be an effective and efficient leader. This documentation of leadership wisdom places the "50 Leadership Keys That Work" at the must have status for your personal library.

—John J. Frattare, Facilitator/Coordinator
Business Men's Fellowship
Rochester, NY

I learned leadership in the United States Marines, first as a follower and then as a leader. I've since learned that leadership principles work everywhere, in every walk of life, whether it's in the marketplace, church world or at home. This is a tremendous opportunity for you to glean almost 50 years of experience from Dr. David Robinson.

He has been a successful leader in business and ministry and now has compiled some his greatest insights and teachings on the subject of leadership. Don't misunderstand, this is easy reading and down to earth, but it absolutely works. You can put it to work immediately in your life, business or ministry. David, job well done, many lives will be changed because of your willingness to share these proven, stabilizing leadership principles.

—Dr. Mark T. Barclay, Living Word Church and
Mark Barclay Ministries, Midland, MI

Since meeting Dr. Robinson, our church and ministry staff has been recharged and redirected by implementing his Coaching4Ministers principles. At a time when I needed a mentor, someone to take me into another dimension, the Holy Spirit placed Dr. Robinson in my life. My ministry has never been the same.

I personally look forward to a deeper walk with God and leading our ministry team into new and exciting realms of the Spirit, ultimately resulting in making true disciples of our church members. Because of Dr. Robinson, we started a Marketplace Ministers class where we train our members to fulfill their calling as Ephesians 4:1 Ministers.

Dr. Robinson's second book contains invaluable leadership lessons that will change many lives and ministries. I strongly urge everyone to purchase this book and not just read it but study it.

—Dr. Daniel Biggs, Senior Pastor, New Beginnings Ministries – Waynesville, MO

David thanks for putting together this easy to read "How to Book" on Leadership Keys. Your unique way of using scriptural principles to point out the lessons makes the information (Golden Nuggets) easy to retain for future use. I know we will use this book as our bible in helping us to be more effective leaders as well as mentoring new leaders.

—Gary Passero, CEO Passero Associates, Rochester, NY

Introduction

On September 23, 1779 during America's war for independence, one of the toughest battles in naval history took place off the coast of Scotland. John Paul Jones, the 32-year-old captain of the American flagship Bonhomme Richard, battled against the far superior 44-gun British Navy frigate Serapis.

After, a ruthless pounding Jones' ship was ablaze and barely above the waterline. Many of his sailors lie dead or wounded across the bloodied decks. The few officers standing by his side were beyond exhaustion. Captain Pearson of the Serapis hailed Jones and inquired politely, "Sir are you ready to strike your colors and surrender?" To which Jones replied, "Surrender sir? I have not yet begun to fight!"

Jones proceeded to lead his decimated sailors in a furious counter attack. He overpowered his enemy and took command of the mighty British frigate – the far superior battle ship. But, on that day the far superior leader, John Paul Jones, would be forever known as a leader who would not quit.

Many times what separates great leaders from all the others is – they just won't quit, in spite of superior odds. Captain Jones turned the tide of America's war for independence because at a critical moment, somewhere deep within his spirit came a decision that quitting was not an option.

I am sure it caught his enemy by surprise and led to a decisive victory in the birthing of our nation. It not only defined the destiny of John Paul Jones, but also defined our nation's destiny – a destiny that has dramatically changed the entire world for over 200 years.

Destiny is about resolve and purpose, how you process information and make decisions. It's about a way of life and not simply ambition and reaching goals. A transcendent God gave every person ever born not only life, but also a destiny. No two are the same everyone is a proto-type. Everyone has a unique fingerprint, eye print and voiceprint. Only a God, beyond human comprehension could give life to over six billion people and make each one different.

Not only are you uniquely formed in your mother's womb, but God gave you a destiny. Webster's Dictionary defines destiny as, "The seemingly inevitable or necessary succession of events possibly caused by a supernatural agency" Webster's New World College Dictionary, fourth Edition 1999.

In some way, perseverance is the key to every great and lasting accomplishment. Great leaders understand this and accept it as their lifestyle. If you are reading this book, it probably means you a leader or at least interested in the subject of leadership.

This book is a compilation of 50 leadership lessons I could say I have learned. However, it is more accurate to say, I am still learning. My life has been framed by the events and experiences God allowed, brought to me, and taken me through. The way I responded and reacted to those events and experiences, defines my life. I failed many times, in so many ways, and in so many roles. But I never failed to get up and go on.

You have a destiny for your life and for your leadership. Much of your success is learning everything you can from your failures. Most of all learn that failure is not permanent unless you fail to get up. Failing is usually preparation for your next success.

May these 50 leadership lessons help you through your failures on your way to fulfilling your destiny as a winner.

"In all things I am more than a conqueror through Jesus Christ my Lord." —Romans 8:37

I have shared these leadership keys as e-Leadership articles over the past five years. The format is the same as when released individually. Some are narratives and others are in outline form. Trust they are valuable to you in your leadership journey.

Lesson 1

Eight leadership keys during transition, crisis or challenge

Two symbols in Chinese represent the word crisis, meaning change with opportunity. If you allow God to develop your leadership during times of crisis, you will have no problem with transition and challenge. The following eight keys will help you and your core leadership teams remain relevant and effective during times that challenge even the best leaders.

Scan the environment

The essence of remaining relevant is having a strategy that is simple, effective and defines the implications of current trends. Those you lead live in the real world. How does your leadership strategy help or hinder them with their marketplace challenges in general and specifically?

Revisit your Mission, Vision and Values often until they are a way of life

Clarity about these is leadership's number one priority. Modeling them consistently is number two and communicating them frequently is number three.

The entire core leadership team must do these with passion, not just the senior leader.

Ban the hierarchical spirit

Structure, systems, and policies are management tools and never canonized or considered unchangeable. People are in strategic leadership positions for leading creative change that fulfills the vision and no other reason. If they cannot do their assignment with excellence and model the values consistently, never put them in a place of leadership.

Establish zero-based programs

Are present programs, events, policies and activities fulfilling our mission and vision? Do they support our values? If not, we need to implement planned abandonment. If you cannot practice abandonment, regardless of how painful it is at times, you will fail when tough times arrive.

Employ the power of language

Speak the words of hope and not words of doubt while not avoiding brutal honesty with present reality. Be a hope dealer not a dream killer. Have few but clear and consistent messages coming from the leadership team. If there is any duplicity among your core leaders, everyone else will know in short order.

Deploy leadership widely

Flatten the flow chart and leadership pyramid. Strategic leadership is about the future, and management is about the present. Both are vital but require different gifts. Great leaders know the difference and deploy leaders appropriately. Strategic leaders spend 80% of their time contributing to the future growth, health and maturity of the organization for which they are responsible.

Lead from the front and not push from behind

Our English word, motivation, comes from two Latin words meaning, "Come from behind and push." Inspire others through your behavior and passion, not wear yourself out pushing people. Trying to inspire unmotivated team members is tiring and bears little fruit. If you have team members who constantly lag behind in attitude or effort at any level regardless of title, position or relationship, it greatly affects the entire organization.

Assess your efforts

Be sure to maintain a well-defined Mission, Vision and Values statements the team refers to often. Create a Strategic Planning Process that provides direction, focus, and serves as a valuable tool for setting goals, creating action plans and measuring results. What cannot or will not be measured, cannot be managed and improved and should be abandoned.

Whether you are going through an uncomfortable transition, a demanding challenge or a threatening crisis, these eight keys will give you and your team relief and confidence. They have helped me as I have developed them through my leadership opportunities since 1966.

Lesson 2

Does setting goals really matter

"If a man proceeds confidently in the direction of his dreams and endeavors to live the life he has imagined, he will meet with success unexpected in common hours." Henry David Thoreau

I meet leaders all the time who have no clearly stated goals. Most are busy managing what is on their radar screen on any given day. Few are able to rise above the pressure of providing solutions while trying to focus on the next step critical to fulfilling their vision. The next step always has a goal or it's not the next step. Setting a goal is good, developing a plan is better, but executing the plan is best.

If you never set realistic goals, give up on your goals in discouragement, or have no clue how goals are set, your system shuts down. In some cases, depression sets in and some leaders even become physically ill. Some prisoners of war, when their hopes for the future were exhausted, they simply lay down and died. Unfulfilled expectations still bring you life's greatest disappointments.

In 1953, Yale University surveyed the graduating class. Of the long list of questions asked, three related to setting goals. "Do you set goals, do you write them down, and do you have a plan to reach them?" Only three percent answered yes to the questions.

Twenty years later, they did a follow up study. As it turns out, the three percent who answered yes to setting goals with a plan to reach them reported they were more happily married, more successful in their carriers, better family life and better health. What was most astonishing was ninety-seven percent of the net worth of the class of '53 was in the hands of the three percent who started setting goals twenty years earlier.

When you have specific goals and accurate feedback about your progress, you open yourself up to a steady flow of opportunities that remains closed to those who have no clear goals and a plan to reach them. Remember, the Holy Spirit did not come to be a laborsaving device but a labor-enhancing Partner. He can only help you reach the goals you properly set.

Do setting goals really matter? Will it make a significant difference in what I am doing? Yes! It did for the class of '53 at Yale. It did for Jesus when the Bible says of Him:

"Who for the prize set before Him, endured the shame of the cross" Hebrews 12:2.

It did for Paul when the Bible says of him: "Fought a good fight . . . finished my course . . . kept the faith" 2 Timothy 4:7.

It mattered for President John Kennedy whose leadership in 1969 sent a man to the moon and brought him home and the technology explosion of that mission changed our world forever.

Five thoughts about goals and goal setting

Goal setting must be a habit that becomes a way of life

Never get involved in any endeavor without setting goals and developing a plan to reach them. Goals are different from hopes, wishes, dreams or good ideas. Goals focus your mind, energy and resources. Goals, properly set, are more likely to happen than wishes, hopes or good ideas.

You need to understand your God-given (R.A.S.) reticular activating system

Your nervous system contains a built-in screening device that will block out or admit information, depending whether that information is important to you. It is a network of cells called the reticular activating system or R.A.S. Its job is determining which of the thousands of sensory messages bombarding you every second get through to your awareness. Without it, we are totally overwhelmed and unable to focus on any one particular thought or task. God has so designed us that it operates without us even being aware of its blessing.

For instances, when mom wakes and dad sleeps on, it is not because the baby's cry is louder than other sounds, but because these sounds are important to her. It works the same for you. Whenever you either declare something to be important because it possesses value or poses a threat, you put your R.A.S. on alert and allow that information through.

When you set a goal, you make a commitment. The number one reason average and poor leaders do not set goals is fear of failure. To avoid failure, they simply avoid setting goals because all goals require commitment. Commitment is the key to successfully reaching your goals.

Commitments do at least three things. First, it means you have a choice and you take the time and fully engage with that choice. Second, it means you are willing to give your best without reservation and pay special attention to the results and progress. Third, you know it requires a significant investment of your time, energy and resources to reap the dividends of your investment.

You must see the "final frame" (results) of the goal

Your action plan may not have all the answers before you take the first step but never let that prevent you from taking the first step. When you set a goal, you tell your R.A.S. and everyone around you, this goal matters. Favor and resources start appearing that were not available before because your R.A.S. screened them out.

However, after you set a goal and commit to its success, the system God created in you helps you see it happen. "We can make our plans (set goals), but the Lord determines our steps (action plans)" Proverbs 16:9 NLT.

Understand the importance of cognitive dissonance

This happens when you try holding two conflicting ideas in your mind at the same time. "How long are you going to waver between two opinions?" I Kings 18:21 NLT.

This state of disharmony (dissonance) has to do with conflicting thoughts (cognition) and always challenging leaders and the leadership they provide. Great leaders know they must make a choice or be frustrated with indecision.

Great leaders inevitably have a strong desire and drive to resolve the conflict, while average to poor leaders are continually frustrated with this mental picture of how things are and how they should be. Whenever your system, your normal routines are thrown out of order, your real leadership ability is brought to light.

It is then the importance of goals becomes evident. As you become dissatisfied with the old, you are energized and motivated by moving beyond the old and resolving this conflict by bringing in the new. With great leaders, this cycle becomes a way of life.

Understand the importance of reciprocal causation

If cognitive dissonance keeps us focused on our goals and moving forward, something called reciprocal causation creates energy and enthusiasm to see our goals become a reality. Great leaders understand, the more you see your goals met and exceeded, the more energy and enthusiasm it creates to see new ones set and the cycle continue. This is the essence of strategic leadership. The moment this cycle stops, you move from creating the future to managing the present.

You stop being a goal-setter and become a problem solver. There are leaders who are great problem solvers and vital to the team. However, someone on the leadership team must lead the effort forward. This kind of leader has an intense desire, based on a vision with specific results focused primarily on accomplishing the goals.

Seven Steps to Achieving Your Goals

Having hopes, dreams, good ideas and even strong desires is not the same as having specific and clearly defined goals. Here are seven steps that will help you in achieving goals if they are properly set.

Write it down

"Write my answer (vision) in large, clear letters on a tablet so that a runner can read it and tell everyone else." Habakkuk 2:2 NLT

Unwritten goals are not goals, simply good thoughts. When you write something down, you declare to yourself and your team - this particular effort matters and we will achieve it with God's help.

Goals must have clarity and specifics.

There is nothing fuzzy about the goals Jesus set for the church in Mark 16 and Matthew 28, His goals answered the Who, What, Why, When, How and Where questions. If yours do not, revise them. If you cannot measure your goals, how will you track the progress, improve the effort, and evaluate the results?

Set some short-term goals

Acts 1:8 says, " . . . first in Jerusalem then . . . " If you do not have short-term wins, you and your team get discouraged at best, demoralized at worst and abandon your long-term goals. Without long-term goals, you lose focus and never realize the ultimate dream.

Make sure your long-term goals stretch you but are attainable.

Nehemiah was a great leader because he understood this balance. Jesus promised he would never give us more than we could bear. If you want to run and finish a marathon, you do not start by running 26 miles the first day. Start small, stay at it and never quit.

Plan for obstacles and setbacks

"We are pressed on every side by troubles, but we are not crushed and broken. We are perplexed, but we don't give up and quit. We are hunted down, but God never abandons us. We get knocked down, but we get up and keep going . . . so that the life of Jesus may be seen in us" 2 Corinthians 4:7-10.

Walking by faith does not mean your life will be free of obstacles and setbacks. It means you know what to do when they come. Do not let a setback stand in the way of your faith to believe your goals are achievable. Just like a good weld, we are always stronger at the broken places. Obstacles will cause you to be more determined or cause you to quit. The Bible says: "The just man falleth seven times but rises again" Proverbs 24:16 KJV.

Track your progress and reward your team

Consistent goal achievers measure the progress along the way, not just at the end. Identify how you do on a daily basis—not just once a month or occasionally. Reward your team and yourself for short-term achievements. Do not wait to throw the big party at the end. Little victories and celebrations keep everyone energized and focused.

Affirm and visualize achieving your goals. The scriptures say about Moses

"He endured seeing Him who is invisible." Hebrews 11:27. The scriptures say of Jesus: "Who for the joy (prize) that was set before Him endured the cross" Hebrews 12:2.

Affirmation is simply confirming the truth of something verbally or in writing. Visualization is the supernatural ability to seeing the victory and achieving the goal before it happens. It is the God-given ability to persevere until your goals are a reality.

How long will it take? Some goals are easily met others are not. Nevertheless, the process is the same. The more you work at it, the better you are in your ability to set achievable goals. It took me 44 years to achieve my educational goals. Many times I felt like giving up but I re-focused and kept going.

Lesson 3
Just do it

This is the famous Nike slogan known around the world. Following through on your commitments should not be a goal to reach for, but a way of life. All of us are disappointed because of unfulfilled commitments.

Unfulfilled expectations bring life's greatest disappointments have been my mantra for years. Many have ideas, a few even have plans, but most average leaders never follow them through to completion. Finishing is not an option for successful organizations. First, it is a discipline then a way of life.

Too many leaders delegate a successful finish to their subordinates because it usually involves too many details. The hope for a successful outcome must not be delegated. It remains every leader's main job. Don't take it for granted, if you do, disappointment is coming.

Place a premium on completion not just action. It must be a core value or it does not happen on a consistent basis. The best strategic planning efforts are worthless without a commitment to finish with the desired results. Action without results produces sweat but not often success.

Senior Leaders are responsible for creating a culture of productivity. Some people have the same position too long. They think their value comes from just showing up and maintaining. Leadership, at any level, is about finishing with the desired results. So much of what is done on a daily basis is disconnected from strategy, action plans or goals. Someone must maintain the present but not the leaders who have the responsibility for creating the future.

Putting a plan in place is easy. Setting a goal is easy. Following through to the finish line is the challenge. Distractions, unanticipated problems, people letting you down and a myriad of other things challenge your best strategies and plans. In spite of that, great leaders "Just do it" they find a way to finish.

Too many leaders kid themselves about how well things are going because they don't want to face present reality. Ninety percent do not set real goals because they have not committed to a strategy connected and driven by goals. If you never commit to a strategy for the future, you are never guilty of not finishing. Being sufficiently challenged means, involvement in something where there is a risk of failure.

The difference between winning and losing is commitment to action and finishing. In our present culture, there are no free passes for those who simply want to try something or just show up. Finishing successfully is the single biggest challenge facing leaders today.

Six steps to finishing with positive measurable results

Identify why finishing your strategy is a problem

Many times, you spend so much energy in meetings, planning, analyzing, and philosophizing, you (with the greatest influence) have little left making sure the plan is completed.

Leaders too often delegate the follow through and move on to what they perceive are more important issues

There is no more important issue than finishing the strategy with measurable and positive results.

Execution of a strategy should be a regular internal discipline, not a tactic used on occasion.

If not, that is why you see so many promises made and so few results delivered. Internal discipline wins every time over external pressure, lack of an action plan and undisciplined efforts.

The better you and your team are at finishing determines the challenges you can undertake

Not every aspect of your strategy will produce the desired results but do not let that hinder you from finishing. Learn from your efforts but, by all means finish!

Make sure you have the right people, in the right place and doing the right things

You can enter the race with an old nag, but if you want to win consistently, you have to develop some thoroughbreds. Ready-made thoroughbreds are usually expensive, hard to find, harder to keep and difficult to keep in line. All great leaders can take an average team member who is highly motivated and turn them into a loyal champion who will help them finish. All finishers are winners, regardless of the score.

Hold people accountable for developing a good strategy (action plan), not just for starting with great enthusiasm, and finishing with measurable-positive results

Make sure they fill the gap between the promises made and the results delivered. If not, check your teaching, training or coaching efforts. Great leaders look in the mirror before looking out the window.

If your leadership efforts survive and thrive during difficult days, they must have an effective, an on-going strategic planning process in place that is coupled with a relentless passion to finish.

"So we built the wall, and the entire wall was joined together...for the people had a mind to work. So the wall was finished in fifty-two days. When our enemies heard...and all the nations around us saw ... they perceived that this work was done by our God." Nehemiah 5:6; 6:15-16

Great leaders are passionately involved in their work. They are honest about present reality for themselves, the effort they lead and the world around them. However, nothing motivates them more and establishes greater credibility than finishing. Many have great ideas, know the right words to say about strategizing and load you up with good information. But, only a few, about three percent, deliver the planned and desired results on time, on budget and in a positive environment. If you are willing to work, not afraid of risk and have an unquenchable passion, you can be in that three percent.

Lesson 4
Seven actions of leaders who make things happen

Leaders function as a strategic leader and utilize teamwork

I see many senior leaders bogged down in day-to-day management and forget their role as a strategic leader. Whatever shows up on their radar screen is where they focus. If you have strategic (future) leadership responsibilities, your primary function is communicating (not managing or controlling) the mission, vision and values. If you don't, who does in the organization you serve? Understanding your team members individually and as a team is your secondary role. Teamwork is your primary way of pursuing the vision and reaching your goals.

Leaders define present reality with brutal honesty

Ministries are full of people who do not want to deal with present reality much less with brutal honesty. The reasons are many. It makes some people uncomfortable; hide or downplay mistakes, avoid confrontation, or simply live in denial are just a few.

As a leader, refusing to define present reality with brutal honesty means, you are not ready to move to the future, whether it is this afternoon, next week, next month or next year. You cannot paint a picture for what you want (called vision) if today's reality is vague in your mind or the team's.

Leaders establish clear and compelling goals

I have coached many leaders who, when we start talking about goals and strategy, cannot tell me what the next step is as it relates to their vision and why. Do you wake up every day and feel like you are facing 50 gorillas? You cannot deal with all of them but without clear and compelling goals, you will burn out trying.

If you have more than two to three new organizational goals for the year, you have too many. If everything is a priority, then nothing is a priority. Months and years pass without progress because the details hold you hostage. You have managers for handling the details, as a leader stay focused on the future. Every day, week and month should have goals that support your annual goals. If they are not compelling to you, you can be sure they are not for your team.

Leaders make follow-through a way of life

Setting clear and compelling goals matters little if no one takes them seriously. Everyone may agree that it's a great goal but it will not happen unless you hold someone accountable for the results.

If, there are no consequences for lack of follow through and desired results, then do not expect much to change. However, before you start holding people accountable make sure they understand the task; are trained until they perform it competently; are given adequate resources; and kept inspired by you, their leader. Only then do you have the right to hold them accountable for the agreed upon results.

Leaders grow well-rounded team members

Being a positional, appointed or elected leader and being a leader who builds a great team following a compelling vision are not the same. Developing emotionally mature team members has never been a greater challenge for leaders. The pace and pressures of life for everyone has intensified. You need to spend at least 40% of your available time developing the top 15-20% of your leaders in the qualities found in Luke 2:52, *"And Jesus increased in wisdom, in stature, and in favor with God and Man."*

If you want to develop this type of team member, you must find time apart from the task. Relationships built only around the task usually lead to burnout or bailout. If your team members know you trust them and believe in them for who they are, not just for what they can do, most will give you 100% regardless of the effort or the demands you place on them.

Leaders understand rewards and sanctions and get them right

Do not pass these out until your team understands them and can perform the task competently; then coach them to excellence through rewards and sanctions. Telling someone to do something is not the same as teaching, training and coaching. Many times, you pass out rewards and sanctions prematurely, usually with little if any long-term results. Make your standards and expectations for both clear, firm and fair.

Leaders don't kid themselves

Shakespeare said, "To thine own self be true." Without emotional maturity, you are never honest with yourself or others. If you or those on your team do not follow through with the plan then do something about it. One of the worst things you can do is kid yourself into believing you can be a great leader without follow-through.

Being a good leader is not the same as giving leadership where following through is never an option. Great leaders come to grips with their own weaknesses. They deal with them honestly and move on. However, lack of follow-through should never qualify as an acceptable weakness. Do not tolerate it for yourself or anyone on your team. If you do, do not be disappointed when your goals are not met.

The Apostle Paul said, *"I have finished my course."* You may not have finished every race just finish the one you are running now. Forget the past and focus on today, the only day that matters.

Yesterday is a cancelled check and tomorrow is a promissory note.

Lesson 5
Selecting the right people

Choosing the right team members is the key to great leadership. In the last 40 years, there have been over 500 head coaching changes in the National Football League, America's number one professional sport. The Pittsburgh Steelers, winners of more Super Bowels than any of the 32 teams, selected three during those 40 years. They have set the standard in making the right leadership choices in the world of professional sports.

Many things, beyond your control, affect your leadership challenges every day. However, one you can is making the right choice when choosing new team members. As a leader, you have no greater challenge than choosing the right people to help you see your vision become a reality.

Ministries and organizations constantly struggle finding strategic leaders that know how to make good personnel decisions. These decisions must not only address today's challenges but tomorrow's opportunities. You must have both qualities in those you choose to join your team. If you do not pay attention during the selection process, you pay dearly for a long time for a poor selection. Be slow to appoint to avoid having to "dis-appoint" yourself and your team.

Five reasons the wrong people get on your team

We do not know them as well as we think we do

Positive first impressions sometimes cause us to fail being thorough throughout the entire selection process. First Thessalonians 5:12 says, *"Know them which labor among you."* This means know them well not just through a resume or casual acquaintance.

We like them

We want to be liked and feel comfortable around them rather than deal honestly with their skills and ability to follow through and deliver positive results on a timely and consistent basis.

Spirituality is important but should never be an acceptable excuse for not finishing

Jesus said, *"It is finished,"* and the Apostle Paul said, *"I have finished my course."* The more mature a person is the better finisher they are, especially when times are tough and resources are scarce.

Loyalty and trustworthiness are mandatory

For any selection you make, those qualities alone are no guarantee you have made the right choice. They can be qualified and a good person but not the right person.

Great personality, good people skills and high I.Q. are not reliable indicators that a person is a finisher, especially when challenged and over the long haul. In any leadership position, there are non-negotiable elements that determine success and indicate if a person is a finisher. Great leaders always have that discussion before choosing any future team member.

"Unfortunately, too much experience in losing gracefully often lowers the resistance to defeat. Through the years, I have found that between equal teams, the winning formula is a thin margin about which to remain requires fidelity to fundamental principles and a team faith that abhors mediocrity and moral victories. I have often stated that there was never a champion who to himself was a good loser. There is a vast difference between the good sport and a good loser. Many have never experienced the pride of accomplishment which only comes from sacrifice and superior performance."

Red Blaik, football coach at West Point, summer of 1952 in a letter to General Douglas MacArthur.

Five keys to look for when selecting team members

They have no substitute for finishing

Just as there is no substitute for winning, they do not tolerate quitting before the task is complete. They have clarity about the assignment, agreement on the outcomes and deadlines, a commitment to do whatever it takes to win, and the discipline to see it through. You are a winner if you don't quit before you finish. Our world has too many starters and not enough finishers.

They create energy wherever they go

Be careful your leadership does not drain the life out of your team. I am not talking about pep talks, hype and painting inspirational word pictures of what could be. Great leaders through actions and reactions bring life and energy on a daily basis. It's more than having an upbeat personality.

Great leaders believe in their vision, are absolutely certain God picked them to lead the effort, and make no compromises in surrounding themselves with like-minded team members.

They are not afraid to make the tough decisions

Average leaders can make the easy ones. However, it takes great leaders to make the difficult ones and make them while it still matters and get them right most of the time. Leaders who waiver, procrastinate and avoid making the difficult decisions clutter most second and third generation organizations. Don't be one of them. Choose people who have a track record of making the close calls and getting them right most of the time.

They are a team player

The days of the solo superstars are over. Individualism should no longer be tolerated by relevant and cutting edge organizations. To be a good team player you must have a high E.Q. (emotional maturity level). Great team leaders and team members are committed to accomplishing the vision together. Remember, a group working on the same project is not the same as a team all pulling together.

They know how to develop people and build teams

They have a proven track record of getting things done through people. This is fundamental to good leadership much less great leadership. If you can't do this, get out of the way and let someone else lead while you find someone to follow. Don't create roadblocks.

Insecure leaders constantly stifle initiative, creativity and innovation. Many leaders confuse delegation with deferring. They abandon their team members and call it empowerment. If you want to be a great leader, learn the difference and delicate balance between paying attention and micro managing.

When evaluating a possible team member, who fulfills all the basic requirements and looks like a strong candidate, keep in mind what counts, most of all at that point is their track record of finishing. Without verification, the glow of everything else on the resume fades quickly. You don't have to tell great finishers twice, wind their clock every day or constantly stand them up, they just finish what they start every time.

Lesson 6

Three things you must get right when selecting your team

Jesus set the standard; He picked the right team members, though not always the brightest and most skilled. He developed a winning strategy for the assigned mission.

His was evangelism and discipleship so He designed a structure that brought daily operational value. The structure He chose was mission driven - not program driven. His visionary leadership was all about the mission and vision, not the programs to support those.

Programs are needed to advance the vision but they always need more resources and people. Great leaders never allow programs to determine the vision nor clutter the path to fulfilling it. Mission and vision are not about programs but clarity, teamwork and are leveraged through your visionary influence, not your programs. Select the right people before you select the programs.

Select the right team keeping three keys in mind

First, know your evaluation process is accurate and thorough. Second, know how to identify and develop leaders at all levels, leaders who manage well and lead the team into the future. Third, know how to keep the leadership pool filled with new leaders for every generation at every level.

Most ministries and organizations look for great leaders for today's challenges but forget tomorrow's changing opportunities. If you do not seize today's opportunities, they often become tomorrow's overwhelming problems. You may find yourself behind the curve.

Back there it always costs more, efforts are less effective, and substantial change is almost impossible. You can have the right strategy, best organizational structure money can buy, and unlimited resources, but if you do not have a continual supply of the right people, the vision will not happen.

Matching the right people to the right opportunity is a skill all great leaders possess. Sometimes they choose good people, but they are not the right people. Sometimes they need reassigned, replaced or even released if necessary. They must handle today's challenges with an eye on tomorrow if they are of any value to you and the team when tomorrow comes. Tomorrow always comes before most inexperienced or untrained leaders are ready. Note the ten virgins in Matthew 25.

How do you know if you have the right people, doing the right thing, in the right place, at the right time? First, they are committed to you their leader, the vision and the action plan. Second, the team's goals and targets energize and clearly focus their efforts. Third, they constantly develop leaders, not just followers. Fourth, they release the "vision drainers" before too much damage takes place. Fifth, they are low maintenance, self-starters and finishers.

Develop the right strategy (action plan)

When reaching your goals and seeing your vision become a reality, it must be simple, goal-driven, people friendly and connect the vision pursuit to the mission (your purpose). It must be sustainable, achievable and define your direction and focus. It must say who is going to do what by when. Its sum and substance must come from those closest to the action, not from the command center in some distant land or even down the hall.

Your visionary leaders create overall focus and boundaries and design basic strategy. Every supporting team must have their own strategy that compliments and strengthens the corporate strategy. If you are struggling with developing a strategy for your ministry or organization:

Email c4mcoach@gmail and request my *"Nine-Step Strategic Planning Process"* outline.

Great leaders bring operational value on a daily basis using the correct strategy

If you are not consistently reaching your goals, change the way you are organized or change the way you operate. The connection between your team members, your strategy (action plan) and the way you operate (the way you go about your daily tasks) must be strong, clear and simple.

Your strategy defines where you are going, guides your team members and determines your structure (daily operation) that creates the path to completion. Success in finishing, whether daily, annually, or the *final frame* of your vision is determined by getting those three steps right.

Get your core leaders together for a checkup and ask the following questions

Do you and your team members have the skills to competently serve your organization, finish the job and win? Every team lacks in some areas.

Ask yourself, am I willing to do whatever it takes to close the gap?

How well does everyone understand and passionately support the Mission, Vision, Values and Strategy?

What adjustments need made?

How will you handle those who cannot or will not make the needed adjustments?

How well do you understand the beliefs and behaviors of those on your team?

Do they place a high value on finishing; maintaining a winning attitude and vocabulary; have a willingness to stay on a continuous learning and improvement curve, and display emotional maturity while under pressure?

Is every team member committed to personal growth to the team and teamwork for delivering measurable results? If not, you need to change the culture or find new team members.

If you want to finish and finish well, see your vision become a reality, do not ignore the reality of these four checkpoints. Let them be speed bumps in your daily operation and energizing points helping you create momentum and success. Great leaders don't stop until they finish.

Lesson 7

Thirteen mistakes leaders make and how to avoid them

Mistakes—we all make them. I learned more from my mistakes and failures than my successes. The key word is learned. If you learn and move on, chances are you will not repeat them.

The Bible says, *"A just man falls seven times but he rises again"* Proverbs 24:16. One difference between winners and losers is winners keep getting up after they fall. If you fall, it means you had to be somewhere to fall from. People who never try are either fearful of risks or what others think. They never have to worry about falling - or succeeding either for that matter. Mistakes are never final unless you refuse to learn, get up or try again.

Some mistakes I made and how you can avoid making them

You refuse to accept personal responsibility for all your actions

Great leaders always look in the mirror first before assigning blame. They have enough self-confidence to admit their weaknesses and mistakes.

Self-confidence and weak excuses is a formula for failure. People follow those they respect.

You earn respect by accepting personal responsibility for your mistakes, not just successes.

You fail in developing people and building them into a team of confident, competent, responsible and mature adults

The test of your leadership is not what can do but what you empower your team to do. People usually do what you expect and inspect provided you have taught and trained them well.

When developing an organization you don't have time, energy or resources to "re-parent" future leaders. If they do not have the basics of character, dependability and loyalty by age 25, on-the-job training seldom works. Teach your future leaders to be problem-solvers not problem-givers. They must learn early that challenges flow downhill and not uphill. Until you develop this skill in your team members, they remain a liability and never become an asset.

You mistake controlling people instead of influencing results. The challenge of increasing effectiveness and efficiency understands how and why people behave as they do in critical situations

Performance improves in direct proportion to your ability to influence their thinking - not control their behavior. Poor behavior is always a product of poor thinking.

Great leaders influence the two questions team members think about constantly. Can I succeed? Where is the value for me? These two questions determine their willingness to face new challenges and improve daily performance. If you do not influence their thinking, you can be sure others will.

You compromise leadership and team loyalty

When second tier and future leaders refer to senior leaders as "they," they have joined the wrong team. Every team member must see themselves as vital to success and part of the leadership team.

No, "they" should exist within any organization. Make sure you and your teams maintain a healthy attitude and enough relational equity sufficient for success and significance.

You lead everyone the same way

Leaders who try leading every team member the same way or only use one method should expect disappointment. Great leaders understand the essential differences in the personalities, strengths and weaknesses in individuals, adjust their leadership style accordingly. While not compromising expectations and goals, great leaders learn a one-size-fits-all leadership style seldom produces desired results.

Leadership, at some point, must be a one-on-one proposition. If you say something to an audience of one, no one doubts whom you aim at. This clarity allows you to quickly get at the root of the problem, deal with it honestly and move on.

You forget the importance of results

Leadership is about results - not keeping the troops busy and happy. If you can't measure it, how do you determine success? You should evaluate your leaders on their ability to execute change and produce positive results.

The more team members understand the cause-and-effect relationship between what they do and the desired results, the more effective and efficient they are in fulfilling the vision. Only by constant attention, adequate teaching and competent training will everyone on your team know how they contribute to the "bottom line."

You focus on problems rather than goals relating to the vision

Great leaders constantly move away from the problems and toward the future. They do this by understanding the power of creativity. Instead of sending the hungry crowds away, Jesus (consummate leader) said, *"What's for lunch?"* The Disciples (managers) said, *"Only a few loaves and fishes."*

Too many leaders act like non-swimmers, always thrashing about fighting the water. The more they do this, the quicker they drown. Creativity is the ability to understand your present reality and use it to your advantage.

Stop draining your energy by focusing on the problems. You will be depressed and your team de-energized. Great leaders do not ignore problems; they just make them the focus of someone else and stay focused on the goals.

You try to be a friend and the leader at the same time

You must create some separation between yourself and those you lead or a spirit of familiarity may set in. This is not a separation in geography or position but one of respect and attitude.

Leading effectively means, you never put the individual above the team and its mission. You are always concerned about the individual but never sacrifice concern for the team. When individuals are hurting, they need belong on the sidelines getting help, not still playing the game. If they remain as active players, they will hurt the team.

You fail to define expectations

Unfulfilled expectations still bring life's greatest disappointments. Your ability to attract and retain valuable people increases in direct proportion to your ability to define expectations from the beginning. Good people who cannot find fulfillment and value associating with you and your team will not stay with you for the long haul. If they stay around too long they damage the team and diminish your leadership in the eyes of the team.

Clearly presented values, mission and vision statements speak loudly about the caliber of your leadership. Values are a source of confidence as long as the stated values match the behaviors modeled by you and your leadership team.

You fail to provide adequate teaching, training or coaching

There are only three reasons why people do not perform up to expectations. First, they lack clarity about the task. Second, they do not know how to perform competently because of inadequate training. Third, they simply don't want to or hindered by something beyond their control.

Leaders must understand the difference between teaching, training and coaching. Teaching is in the classroom. Training is on the job and coaching is on the sidelines providing options. You teach to know, you train to competency, and coach to excellence. Training is not providing more knowledge—but using knowledge as a tool.

Training aims at competent action and evaluating what a person can do with what they know. Confused people usually do not, or should not, take action. Vince Lombardi said, *"It is very hard being aggressive when you are confused."* Coaching these kinds of people will wear you out.

You condone incompetence

In training, do not punish the learner. Never reprimand a person until they have demonstrated the ability to meet expectations. Great leaders refuse accepting second best and keep returning to education and training issues until team members display competence with consistency.

Coaching leaders act quickly and consistently before the problem grows. Very little gets better with age. The moment a lack of competence appears, don't wait; clarify and confront if necessary. Good coaching and clarity eliminates the need for confrontation most of the time. If the situation calls for confrontation, here are seven guidelines that will help you:

1. Never, confront in anger.
2. Do it in private.
3. Do it immediately—provided you are in control of your emotions.
4. Be specific—separate the person from any and all undesirable behavior.

5. Use adequate and accurate information and pre-determined expectations.
6. Be clear about how you feel and fair in your judgments.
7. Provide redirection with adequate coaching.

You recognize only the top performers

All great organizations build on good middle producers and a few top performers. Every team member not only deserves, but also requires recognition individually and for team results. Most people scramble for recognition and many feel starved for it.

Recognition and respect are foods for every man's spirit. Well-fed teams seize every opportunity provided by great leaders to fulfill their destiny. That never happens without senior leaders recognizing and respecting all team members, not just the top performers.

You try manipulating people instead of inspiring them

Essentially every leadership effort falls into one of two categories, manipulating and using people or building people through inspiration.

Manipulation is using fear or incentives for producing short-term results without concern about the long-term problems it creates. You do this by arranging circumstances designed to bribe or force team members to perform.

Great leaders know how to inspire people to achieve using their inner strengths, while bullies use fear and threats.

Productivity reflects the individual's confidence in God, himself, his team and the service they provide. Overuse of fear, intimidation, and rewards destroys these essential characteristics.

As a result, team members feel used, loss of self-esteem and respect for their leaders, and possibly resentment for the organization they serve, if not corrected.

"The man who makes no mistakes does not usually make anything." —Edward John Phelps

"An expert is someone who knows some of the worst mistakes that can be made in his subject and manages to avoid them." —Werner Heisenberg

Lesson 8

Whether you lead a church, para-church or a marketplace ministry, the calling of all leaders is extending the Kingdom by the leadership they provide. Their first priority is the emotional and spiritual health of themselves, the team they lead and the marketplace effort (ministry) that looks to them for leadership.

When determining the health (spiritual and emotional) of the church you pastor, organization or marketplace effort you lead, stay focused on three areas:

Healthy managers (pastor) their marketplace effort

Healthy leaders live a balanced life. God does not want you burning out or rusting out. Fulfilling your destiny requires neither. Healthy leaders model the Apostle Paul's admonition *"Follow me as I follow Christ"* in the pursuit of their God-given destiny, partnership with their spouse, family leadership responsibilities, their example in the public arena, and the way they approach their assignment.

They are disciples' of Christ, faithful following learners and students of the Word rightly dividing the Truth, passionate proclaimers of the Gospel message, and sensitive to the leading of the Spirit on a daily basis.

Healthy strategic leaders lead healthy organizations and consistently ask?

Is our marketplace ministry philosophy and method of leadership based on a solid biblical foundation, traditions of men or anti-biblical marketplace pressures?

Are we committed to a sacred calling (not just a job) that goes beyond being a private chaplain for meeting all the felt and expressed needs of those we lead at the expense of developing effective marketplace disciples?

Do we see ourselves responsible for identifying the Mission, Vision, Values of our organization and serving as transformational leaders for their fulfillment?

In Christian organizations, does the entire leadership team embrace every member of our organization as a Spirit-born, Spirit-filled, and Spirit-gifted leader who God expects me (us) to teach, train and coach to fulfill their God-given destiny?

Only healthy team members populate your marketplace effort

They are genuine converts, living (daily) a separated lifestyle, and fully connected to the culture of our day—but not influenced by it. They have a passion for the Word of God as evidenced by their study, meditation and practice in everyday life. They are given to a lifestyle of prayer; warriors that know how to do battle and win with the truth.

They are committed to discipleship not just believing, as evidenced by a Spirit of faith, Spirit of love and a Spirit of excellence in every area of their life and ministry assignment. They are willing evangelists to the unbelievers God places in their life by Divine appointment.

They are a submitted and humble follower of Christ as evidenced by their behavior towards those He has placed over them in the Lord and the marketplace. They are committed to the Mission, Vision, Values and Strategy of their church and organization or marketplace ministry.

Too many are trying to get smart before they get healthy. No matter how smart using the latest methods and ideas, without emotional and financial health, your marketplace ministry is ineffective at best or eventually dies at worst.

Lesson 9
Developing accountable leaders

Do you want effective leadership influence during your lifetime and beyond? Then design a process for developing leaders within a culture of accountability. You can adopt the best standards of behavior but if your leaders lack "know how" or are unwilling to clarify (confront, if necessary) vital issues and under-performing team members, little else matters.

You can have the best mission, vision, and values statements coupled with an outstanding strategy, but if your leadership does not know how or fails to communicate them well, little else matters.

You can give out certificates, awards and incentives, but if your leaders do not know how or fail to use them to align team members' efforts to goals and values, those documents are simply good statements but do little in guiding the efforts of the leadership team.

Developing leaders in an accountability culture is not an option but a priority. Jesus thought so when pouring most of his time and effort into twelve men, while the crowds begged for His attention and time. Many say it is a priority but fail to invest significant time and energy into building an accountability culture.

Developing leaders and leadership accountability must not be an occasional event, but an ongoing process. Your process must not be vague, random or soft. If it is, do not expect much to change.

No organization can be relevant and last for generations without great leadership. You cannot have sustainable and measurable growth without well-trained, accountable, and passionate leaders at every level in every generation.

Team members seldom leave their ministry (assignment). They leave or quit their leaders. Your role as a leader must go beyond solving today's problems. You must develop an accountability culture that keeps them coming back and reporting for duty even when times are tough and the journey seems long.

How do you develop leaders that hold themselves accountable and their team?

A senior leader must take passionate ownership of the process or it will not happen. Even if that leader delegates much of the process, he or she must initiate the process, pay attention, participate periodically, and celebrate the results.

All present and future leaders must go through your training regardless of history or success elsewhere.

Allow leaders to help design their own training. Allow them to express areas of concern and need for help. Canned programs are rarely successful or sustainable.

Leadership development must connect to the ministry's overall vision and individual performance goals. If they do not see it, they will not buy into it with enthusiasm.

What are the components of a good Leadership Development Process?

Select a qualified and passionate individual to build a team and coordinate this effort. They must understand their mission is providing trained and equipped leaders to achieve the organization's goals and vision.

Teach future leaders to *know* first. Develop a curriculum with learning objectives that turn out leaders with the skills necessary to win at any leadership level. Provide some useable "takeaways" immediately.

Train them for *competency*. Provide significant learning opportunities that are relevant, practical, and focused on positive outcomes. Remember, even little win produces confidence and competence increases the chance of winning often.

Practice *saturation communication*. At times, you can provide too much information but you can never over communicate. Saturate your organization with accurate, adequate and relevant information about your Leadership Development Process especially the benefits. "People buy benefits, not products."

Do not forget the *social aspects* of your process. The leader sets the pace, atmosphere, themes, agenda and activities for each session. Have fun and make it enjoyable. Great leaders always "lighten the load" and make the journey enjoyable. People look earnestly for those kinds of leaders to follow.

Logistics, the Leader is responsible for the facilities, equipment, materials, social aspects (food and fellowship) and cleanup afterward.

Accountability, your leadership development team must provide key leadership concepts at every session and easily understood and executed by all future leaders. They must monitor assignments and progress during and after the sessions. Expectations need evaluated so *accountability* becomes a way of life, not a discussion at an annual performance review.

Summary: Avoid creating "look-alike" leaders. Every future leader brings his or her personality, passion and effort to the team. Treat everyone equally but do not treat everyone the same—teams are made of individuals—not clones.

You must bring consistency and continuity based on a foundation of trust, personal accountability and best leadership practices that are vital to success.

Sustainable efforts never take place without a culture of love, faith and excellence. A great culture out-performs a great strategy every time.

A great leadership culture combined with a clear Mission, compelling Vision, and well-planned

Strategy produces winning teams for today and a lifetime.

Lesson 10
Twelve characteristics of great team leaders

The definition of a team is this: "Three or more people focused on the same purpose with clarity of vision and total commitment to the same goals and results." This is different from a group of people working on the same effort.

Compelling vision—a mental image of the expected results. Leaders must know how to create the vision statement, cast the vision consistently, and show passion for the vision at all times. If the vision is not compelling, the energy of the team is little if any at all.

Telescopic eyes—always keeps the big picture in view. Strategic leaders take an occasional look through the microscope but primarily watch the big picture. You need both but you do not want the one driving the bus just watch the road ahead—you need them out front determining the way forward.

Creative—always finding new ways to be effective and efficient in solving problems. Leaders who are managers are great at solving problems. Strategic leaders show them how to be efficient and effective.

Focused—knows how to identify, focus and laser in "what to do next." Not, what to do next in managing what already exists, but what to do next in creating what does not exist.

Decision maker—not afraid to "pull the trigger" after reasonable analysis and investigation of possible solutions. They do not continue going around the mountain discussing, they make the best possible decision and move on.

Control—has a high level of emotional maturity and "stays cool under fire." They are not rattled easily and do not make the wrong decision. They keep their team at ease and the atmosphere positive.

Handles pressure—not overwhelmed by multiple tasks and conflicting ideas. A person who can only handle one thing at a team should not be leading. The ability to hold two thoughts at the same time, especially conflicting thoughts, is one mark of a great leader.

Trustworthy—keeps their word and is always building relational equity. Honesty is telling the Truth, integrity is telling the whole Truth all the time.

Sense of humor—does not take him or others too seriously. Don't hang around leaders who don't laugh very much. They usually end up making you cry.

Maintains a continual learning curve—for himself, and for all his team members. Some leaders have a lifetime of one year's experience twenty times. Great leaders have twenty years of growing experiences one year at a time. Which would you rather serve?

Encourager—Dallas Willard said, "Man's greatest need and highest achievement." You cannot over-encourage people. However, you can surely discourage them if you pass out affirmations like those that you throw around manhole covers.

Models values—his and the ministry he serves. Never preach the values you never model. Your actions must match your articulation or your preaching is in vain.

Summarize where you may need to improve.

Lesson 11
21st century leadership challenges

Think Globally

Globalization is more than a buzzword – it is a reality every leader must address or accept the fact your ability to compete is almost non-existent. Your little corner of the world is now on the GPS of millions who visit you on Google Earth almost every day. The days of avoidance and compliance are over.

Anticipate and seize relevant opportunities

Opportunities come once in a lifetime and you must address them during the lifetime of that opportunity. Abraham Lincoln said, "Everything comes to those who wait but, only things left by those who hustle."

Create shared vision

Your vision must become Team's vision. If not, your vision is only going as far as you can push it. Do not think for a minute that everyone on your team does not hopes and dreams for their own life. You must find a way to incorporate that into *Our Vision* or the energy level remains low because synergy is absent. Momentum requires both.

Develop and empower present and future leaders

The days of *command and control leadership* have vanished. If you do not empower your team, the better members find a way to leave you. People, never quit their team, they quit their leader.

Build teams and pursue vision through teamwork

The days of solo superstar performers are finished. Teamwork is no longer an option but the only way to function in our high tech and fragmented world. Loners or emotionally immature team members cannot be tolerated you either fix them or release them. The longer they stay – the longer the team suffers.

Embrace change as a way of life

Change should not be an interruption. Great leaders change when they do not have to but they know the time is right. Good leaders change when the handwriting is on the wall and time is running out. Poor leaders try to change when it no longer matters and has no effect on the future.

Celebrate diversity and value everyone

Do not just celebrate diversity embrace it at every opportunity possible. Team members should not be copies, but prototypes. You do not need two of the same—one is not necessary. Everyone has value and great leaders know how to find it. If you cannot, release them and let them serve a leader who can. Even your enemies have value - they keep you focused.

Continually challenge the process without derailing it

Be content, but never be satisfied with how things are. If you are not constantly looking for a better way, you should be managing and not creating the future.

Stay current with information and communication technology

Today's generation read little that is not on their I-pad, I-phone, Laptop or some other digital device. If you are not up to speed your days for leading in today's market are over. If you think, otherwise you are kidding yourself.

Create value for internal and external stakeholders

Increasing share value for the stockholders in the marketplace, or attendance and budgets in the Church world, as the only way to increase value may seem unfair but it is a reality today's leaders face every day. It needs to change and the coming generation must change it or the pressure continues to build on every one.

Remain on a personal and organizational learning curve

Maintain a steep learning curve or lose the race in today's world. Learning is more than an accumulation of the facts. Proverbs 4:7 says, *"Wisdom is the principle thing; therefore get wisdom. And in all getting, get understanding."* Today's western culture is mostly about getting things and very little about getting wisdom. The entitlement society is in full swing. We need leaders who have more than an Ivy League degree – we need some with wisdom for the days ahead.

Consistently sow the seeds of your vision into the soil of your values

Vision, without clear values seldom finds fulfillment. Values, without vision is a contented life without significance. If your vision is not happening—check your values they could be starving the seeds of your vision.

Lesson 12
Leadership's greatest challenge

Astronaut James Irwin said, "You might think going to the moon was the most scientific project ever, but they literally 'threw us' in the direction of the moon. We had to adjust our course every ten minutes and landed only fifty feet inside of a 500-mile radius of our target." On that mission, every change, no matter how small, was essential to success.

Resisting change and defending the status quo only proves that you have no intention of changing. Almost everyone favors progress and dreams of how things could or should be. It's change they don't like. Great leaders are not only willing to change, but change is a way of life for them. Good leaders change when they see the light and poor leaders only change when they feel the heat.

Wise leaders are willing to change their minds, their heart and even their behavior when change is uncomfortable. Willingness to change is a sign of strength--not weakness. Fools seldom make changes even when it really matters. Stubborn fools do not hold opinions; their opinions hold them and the entire organization suffers.

Believing in change is not the same as embracing change by making significant behavioral changes. Significant change means changing behavior from the front office to the front line. The mettle of any leadership team is leading change when it makes the most difference, not necessarily when it makes the most sense.

Change is a process, not an event. Change works when all team members are energized, engaged and adequately informed throughout the process. Change seldom happens when managing leaders are in charge because their gifting and nature is maintaining the status quo. It takes strategic [apostolic] leaders who, by gifting, constantly declare war on the status quo.

Changes come in two forms

First, leaders make a declaration or send out an edict calling for change. If you have enough money, power, authority and time, you can effect change without team members' approval, energy or engagement. *"It's my way or the highway"* does not work anymore.

Second, team members make behavioral changes. This requires a lot of relational equity on the part of core leaders and buy-in by everyone. On average, it takes at least 70% of your front-line leaders supporting change once there is 100% consensus by core leaders. If you try implementing change without this kind of support, positive results seldom occur.

What causes a lack of behavioral change? People are seldom the problem but most often get the blame.

Senior leaders create most of the problems preventing change. How? By their lack of leadership in the following four areas:

1. Lack of clarity about the goals and strategy for change. People cannot buy in to what they cannot see or understand. This clarity diminishes in proportion to the distance a person moves away from the core leaders.

2. Lack of commitment and passion modeled by core leaders for the Mission, Vision, and Values of your organization or ministry. If your leaders have not memorized them, they will never be focused and energized by them. You are only passionate about what you truly believe and find worthy of investing your time and energy.

3. Lack of accountability on a regular basis to reinforce positive sustainable results. Without accountability, there is no way to improve, much less change.

4. Lack of trust in the leadership's abilities and decision-making skills.

However, the *Number One Enemy* in making change, seizing new opportunities, and overcoming active inertia is the urgency to protect and maintain what you already have.

Whatever you focus on the most is what you produce the most. It does not matter if it is the past, present, or future. Whether it works or does not work. Whether it is relevant or irrelevant, your focus determines your outcomes, not how many meetings you conduct or how long and detailed your discussions.

Every team member has a responsible role in achieving the goal for making change happen. Everyone must know the following or change is difficult at best or never takes place at worst.

1. Everyone knows the goals for change and can state them clearly.
2. Everyone knows what it will take to achieve success--individually and for the team.
3. Everyone knows the "score" at all times—as a team and for individual efforts.
4. Everyone knows he or she is accountable regularly to his or her leader, his or her team, and most of all themselves.

Lesson 13
Developing leaders vs. gathering followers

Your ability to develop a team of strategic leaders who know how to lead to the future, not just manage the present, is what determines your long-term success as a leader. In order to fulfill your vision, you must be able to guide the way the team works together in order to deliver the desired results. Successful team leadership is the ability of the leader to rally all the team members around the vision and common goals, not because they have to but because they want to.

Forming a team of mentally, emotionally, and spiritually mature leaders is worth your time and effort. The greater challenge is getting them to lay aside personal ambition and ideas for the sake of becoming a team centered only on the mission and vision. A group of followers working on the same effort is different from a team of strategic-thinking leaders focused on the same goals. They are now a team with a clear understanding and commitment to the same outcome-based results.

Independent thinking team members normally focus on their own strengths and abilities. They usually promote their own ideas of what success should look like. Most of the time, this leads to everyone pulling in different directions and momentum is lost, if it was ever there to begin with.

As a leader, your primary task is inspiring individual team members to check their ego at the door and set aside personal agendas. Only then can you cultivate a passion for teamwork, team solutions and team wins. Look at yourself first.

Your top priority as a team leader, leader of leaders and most of all as a senior leader is having your team understand, focus and commit to the outcome-based goals of the mission, vision, values and strategy. Without clarity about these four key elements buy-in by the team and a commitment to teamwork never happens in any significant way.

Developing leaders out of *gathered* followers happens best when working together as a team is the only option. Team dynamics cannot be developed in solo situations. Do not tolerate for long lone rangers, overbearing personalities and divisive behaviors.

As the leader, you must have the emotional strength and maturity to clarify non-productive behaviors in both strong-willed and weak-minded individuals. Somehow, persuade them to see the big picture and how their individual effort is valuable and vital to the team's success. If not, check your leadership skills or release them from your team, no matter how good they are.

Here are five principles critical for developing a team of leaders

1. Provide adequate and accurate information; clarity about desired results and the rationale used to shape your views.

2. Anticipate, surface and resolve conflicts quickly. As the leader, your job is insuring overly competitive or domineering team members do not exploit another's vulnerability when discussing either positive or negative issues relating to the team's on-going efforts or results.

3. Recruit, teach, train and deploy the right team members. Be slow to appoint so you won't have to disappoint. No matter how talented they are if their ego, personality and effort do not complement the team, you must decide what's more important to you—their individual contribution or the team's success.

4. Provide prompt and adequate feedback. Waiting until the annual performance review means many significant coaching opportunities may be lost. Feedback for both individuals and the team as a whole is most effective in written form. And, I don't mean email! Celebrate both the small and big wins on a regular basis.

5. Recognize and deal promptly with those that I refer to as "Vision Drainers." The biggest reason teams not performing effectively and winning often is the emotional maturity of the leader. It often lies in the discomfort and sometimes fears of giving honest feedback

necessary to develop a group of followers into a team of leaders who win on a regular basis.

Remember, leaders who turn followers into leaders on a consistent basis are leaders who know what they are doing and why. Many times, there are those who give promise of being great leaders because of superficial personality and character traits. Intelligence, confidence and the ability to communicate are important. But, having all these doesn't mean you have the emotional maturity and ability to make good judgments, which are invaluable in turning your followers into leaders.

Lesson 14
Do you have a business or a calling?

God has a purpose for you, your business or profession that is greater than profit, employees, customer satisfaction, and sales. It is glorifying the Lord of the Harvest in the marketplace, your place of ministry.

Until Believers influence three marketplace entities, they will never "...*disciple all nations,*" God's original mandate for the Church. You must infiltrate, elevate, and have superior influence in business, government, and educational institutions that forms the marketplace. The Church must provide teaching, training, and coaching for all Kingdom efforts, not just in the Church world.

We must stop compartmentalizing our lives between secular versus sacred. Secular and sacred never existed in my life. You must integrate all your God-given opportunities into a seamless life lived to the glory of God. If your calling is the marketplace, find your purpose for being there and act on it. Your destiny is making a difference for the Kingdom, not just having a job or owning a business to meet your needs.

You can approach your business or job as a Christian in three ways. First, you can be a Christian in a secular business or position. Second, you can operate or work in a Christian business in a secular marketplace. Third, you can have a Kingdom business or position related to Kingdom purposes and committed to Kingdom expansion.

Live for the Five Greats

Your business or position exists for many reasons, but the primary reason is to glorify God and live for the "Five Greats." The Great Commandment in Matthew 22:35-40 based on love; The Great Commission in Matthew 28:18-20 based on obedience; The Great Opportunity in John 4:35 based on discernment; The Great Disturbance in Acts 1:8 and 2:4 based on passion; and The Great Day in I Thessalonians 4:13-18 based on eternal hope. The target must be the whitened harvest fields, not the well-padded pews of a local church building.

Christians should not have to take time off or retire to be in full-time ministry. My business or position *is* my ministry. It is not my total ministry, but should neither my "church work," what I do at the church building, be the sum total of my ministry. Too many are so busy doing church work they have neither the time nor energy for the work of the church which takes place outside the facilities of the local church.

Bi-vocational or part-time ministers are really oxymoron. I should have one calling lived in every area of my life. Where is the church today? Wherever His sanctuaries (you) are located. We do what we do regardless of the location of our calling. We must do it on purpose, with passion, and specificity. "Adam where are you?" "Moses what are you doing here?" As with Gideon, Joshua or the Apostle Paul we must seek God for our purpose, find a voice for doing it, and fulfill our destiny with a bias for action.

Effectiveness, regardless of endeavor or effort, is about relationships. Whom you know gets you into Heaven and everywhere else, you need to be. The Bible says the planning of our days took place before we were born, and our steps ordered of the Lord. If that is the case, how can we have both secular and sacred parts to our lives?

"Jesus doeth all things well..." Mark 7:37. Our significance and success must link us to a spirit of excellence. We can do some things well and even some things with excellence, but the goal of every Christian is catching the spirit of excellence and developing it into a life-style of excellence.

Perfectionism, the motivation to please men is never a goal rather; it is excellence, the inner passion to do our very best with every opportunity to bring glory to the Lord, regardless of our calling.

Excellence is not a goal but a way of life

Excellence is not an option or a goal to reach for; it must be a way of life. I Corinthians 10:31 says *"...whatever you do, do to the glory of God."* It is not doing a secular duty in a Christian way; it is offering up to the Lord everything you do as a sacred and sacrificial offering to the Lord. He is always worthy of our best efforts regardless of the task.

Our ministry (business or position) should reflect this spirit of excellence. Our sales should be honorable and effective. Financial affairs should be honest and without question. Profit performance outstanding, reflecting our Kingdom commitment and God's favor. Our technology should be current, innovative and appropriate.

Our employment practices must be exemplary. The size of our business or position impact is ultimately up to God. However, the standard by which we operate is our responsibility and should be high and without compromise.

The purpose of our business or leadership impact is creating wealth for expanding His Kingdom. Value determines wealth and wealth is what others are willing to pay for it. Wealth was God's idea and has been in place since He created the world. Someone once said if the wealth of the world's resources (timber, minerals, land, manufacturing, etc.) sold on the open market it would make every person on this planet a billionaire six times over.

God created value and wealth at creation and He gives his children the power to get it and use it to establish His covenant by extending His Kingdom on earth. Too many believe God for miracles when He is saying, "Go to work!" The Hebrew words for work and worship are very similar. God's intention was that our work would be our worship and our worship would be our work. Worship must be more than a song and only given in the church house or behind closed doors.

The Genesis 1:26-31 passage provides a fundamental theology for work and business. Business should never be a means to an end. God gave Adam and Eve the task of managing His creation and instructed to "subdue" and make use of it. God is always about creating value and filling needs. Exploit the potential God has put in you. Adam and Eve were not only given management responsibilities, they were to master (dominate) all of God's creation. Their leadership potential was to create a bright future for all His creation.

In Genesis 1:31 God said all this "was good." It was after the Fall that fallen mankind corrupted everything, including God's business model. God never condemned business, only corrupt businesspersons. Why did God include a business model in creation?

Four reasons God used a Business model in creation

First, to create wealth as a means of providing for Kingdom citizens called to Kingdom building and expansion. He could have provided a steady stream of miracles and provisions, i.e., ravens, cruse of oil, manna in the wilderness, water from a rock, turning tap water into wine, money in a fish's mouth and feeding 5,000 men plus wives and children from a little boy's lunch. Instead, He chose to do most of His providing for mankind through the natural means of work, our worship to Him, not a drudgery to avoid or retire.

Second, business creates relationships whereby God can display and demonstrate His grace in and through the lives of those devoted to Him. The Ephesians 4:1 ministers many times are able to be in places the Ephesians 4:11 ministers may not be welcome, gifted or called to serve.

Third, business was part of the New Testament Church. The Holy Spirit did not come to be a laborsaving device but a labor-enhancing partner. Lydia the merchant in Acts 16, James and John the fishermen, Luke the physician, and Paul the apostle were all beneficiaries of the ministry of the Holy Spirit in the marketplace.

In fact, I believe Paul's ministry never really took off until he created value in the marketplace with Pricilla and Aquila in Acts 18.

Fourth, Jesus was a small business owner most of his life. He recruited His first team for world evangelism from the marketplace. Six entrepreneurial ladies provided most of the support for His three-and-a-half-year itinerant ministry. There must be a message for today's church in there somewhere.

Today's church will see impact in the marketplace, government, and education in direct proportion to the value they bring to those arenas on a consistent basis. It will come from Ephesians 4:1 leaders developed by Ephesians 4:11 leaders to be

Disciples of Christ: called, committed and empowered to be Kingdom builders fulfilling their God-given call.

I am often asked what I think is the number one hindrance to world evangelism. After four-plus decades of ministry in the church and the marketplace, I answer without hesitation; the division men have created between clergy and laity, the called and the un-called, sacred and secular, full-time, part-time and other non-biblical classifications. This classification is the mind-set of too many Christians and traditional church leaders.

None of these classifications is Biblical. Even a cursory study and elementary understanding of scripture reveals God's original intent and continuing desire is to have a kingdom of priests delivering the Gospel with Holy Ghost power to the entire world, resulting in the discipling of entire nations.

Would the real ministers please stand up

We need to develop a Biblical theology for ministry where Christ is Lord of the Marketplace, Governments, and Education, not just the Church. I dare say that Christ is not really Lord of many local churches, and that is why He is not Lord of the marketplace, the educational, and government arenas where the church is located ninety percent of the time.

Ephesians 4:1 says, *"Therefore I, a prisoner for serving the Lord, beg you to lead a life worthy of* *your **calling**, for you have been **called** by God"* NLT. I believe this applies to all ministers, not just those in the Church structure. Those with the gifts of Ephesians 4:11 are called out of all the called ministers to equip the Ephesians 4:1 minister for the work of the ministry where God has called them, not just for church work where they attend. The "saints" of Romans 1:7 is what sets the precedent for Romans 12:1-2 and Ephesians 4:1.

All called ministers were *"...created in Christ Jesus to do good works, which God prepared in advance for us to do" Ephesians* 2:10. The implications should be obvious. First, they were prepared in advance without the input or approval of man. Second, they are for us to do not just meet and talk about. Third, He has given us (all called ministers) everything for life and godliness, not just a select few.

We should not stop short in teaching the priesthood of all believers and the need for a fully empowered priesthood, not only in the Church, but also in the marketplace, where most Christians live their lives and battle for the Kingdom. Let me elaborate in three specific areas.

Ministry should not be a bi-vocational issue.

All of life is sacred for the Christian. Someone once said, "When is a bird most glorifying to God, when it is flying, singing or when it is preaching?" Answer, what glorifies God most is not the essence of the activity but whether it is what He wants me to do now.

What were you made to do is your calling. All Christians have a calling, a God-given destiny, but not enough to change the marketplace significantly. *"To all in Rome who are loved by God and called to be saints . . ."* Romans 1:7 literally, it means *"holy ones."* Every Christian is sanctified set apart for God's purpose and calling. Tie this to Romans 8:28 *"...called according to his purpose."* We must stay focused on the unlimited application of God's call. Christians by definition are called Christians or they are not Christians at all. Being sanctified, holy and acceptable is not the call or status of a select few but the mandate for everyone in the Body of Christ.

The call is always *to* something and *for* something. That something is your destiny, not just your service to the Body of Christ and witness in the marketplace. Your destiny will always be bigger than you are and outlast your lifetime. If not, maybe what you have is only a position, a business or a passionless pursuit you call a job.

Each calling is just as significant as every other calling. The idea of degrees or levels of calling are a breeding ground for depression, division and pride. If God has called you to business, government, or education, no other calling would be a promotion but a step down. After all these years, I am still trying to understand what people mean when they say they are quitting their job and going into *"full-time ministry"*.

Your Kingdom business or position must have purpose and intentionality.

Your life's calling must have a purpose and sense of mission beyond making a profit and consuming more earthly goods. God is a God of purpose. Everything He ever did, He did on purpose. Scriptures abound that support this premise, i.e. Genesis 1:26, Jeremiah 29:11, Romans 8:28-29, Ephesians 1:11.

Your business or profession exists to glorify God. It exists to contribute to the major Kingdom building activities that support this purpose. If you are an owner or an employee, your efforts are to bring glory to your God. Man to simply gain wealth or control others did not create business. God instituted it with the Divine purpose of edifying humankind and ultimately bringing glory to his Creator.

How do you discover God's Kingdom purpose for your marketplace calling? The Bible is filled with instructions. First, we submit to God and those He has put in authority over us. God always reveals His will to those willing to do it and understand the following three things.

His purpose revealed in his Word.

"The secret things belong to God, but the things revealed belong to us and to our children forever that we may be able to follow all the words of this law." Deuteronomy 29:29

"He has shown you O man what is good. In addition, what does the Lord require of you? To act justly and love mercy and walk humbly with your God." Micah 6:8

"All scripture is God-breathed and is useful for teaching, rebuking, correcting and instructing in righteousness so the man of God may be thoroughly equipped for every good work." 2 Timothy 3:16-17

"His divine power has given us everything we need for life and godliness through our knowledge of him who called us by his own glory and goodness. Through these he has given us great and precious promises so, that through them you may participate in the divine nature and escape the corruption by evil desires." 2 Peter 1:3-4

The knowledge that God's will for your business is revealed when He knows you are ready, willing, and obedient to His word, His will and His way—not just committed to being a good businessman, government official or professor.

God does not reveal His will to those who want to know what it is before they decide if they want to do it. You must follow a clear path in fulfilling God's destiny for your life and ministry. Submission without reservation, revelation through His Word, clarity of the next step, and obedience without question are required before a manifestation of His will arrives.

This was Paul's point in Romans 12:1-2. You must understand God's general will for mankind and then His specific will for your own life. You must surrender and embrace it with passion. As you go through this process (not event), you are changed to conform, not only to His image but also to His will. You will have wisdom, knowledge and understanding through the opportunities and experiences only He can provide.

Your steps are ordered and not random. You are not a victim of circumstances but more than a conqueror, but only through Him. Too many trust God in church but try to do it on their own in their business or Kingdom position.

The purposes and plans of God are spiritually understood

They do not always make sense to the natural mind and feel comfortable to the flesh. If you want to know what the *"hope of your calling"* is for your life and business, develop the following six disciplines in your daily walk with God.

First, pray. Prayer is not a matter so much about position as it is about the attitude of your heart. Prayer is not a scheme we use to influence God to allow us to have our own way. Neither is it a scream where we are trying to get God's attention so we can inform Him of our situation as if He did not know.

Prayer can be many things, but primarily it is an on-going conversation. It is not a one-way monologue where one person does all the talking. As we pray we understand, not just the will of God, but also the heart of God. What comes from the heart goes to the heart. What comes from the mind seldom reaches the heart.

Second, read, study, memorize and confess the Word of God. Live a life saturated by the Word of God. The Truth of God's word not only sets you free from sin, but also frees you to understand God's purpose and plan for your life and business. The facts of life are true but they are not always the Truth.

Truth always overrides the facts. It is not "you shall know the facts and the facts will make you free," but *"you shall know the truth and the truth shall make you free."* It is one thing to be set free (an event) from sin and its effects but quite another to be made free (a process) to know the heart of God and all that He has planned for us before we were even born.

Third, hang out with balcony people and avoid basement people. Balcony people have an elevated view of life. They can see a long way and look over a lot of stuff from that perspective. Basement people cannot see very far, and the view from down there is cluttered with things that hinder them from seeing what God has for them, their loved ones, and their business or profession.

Find other business people or professionals who know they are called to extend God's kingdom. You usually do not find these people hanging out in the basement, be it in the church or marketplace. Both have basements you must avoid.

Fourth, be a reader because great leaders are readers. Stay informed about what is going on around you, in your world and the rest of the world. The sons of Issachar *"understood the times and knew what to do."* God is at work everywhere all the time and He wants you to know what He is doing, why He is doing it, and how you and your business should be involved. Uninformed leaders are, at best a distraction, and at worst a detriment to the Kingdom.

Fifth, keep a journal. All great leaders were writers even if not published. They recorded the significant events and activities of their lives. Putting your thoughts on paper helps crystallize what God is saying to you and reveals how you really feel about it.

Sixth, have personal mission, vision, and value statements. If you do not understand God's specific purpose and plan for your life and how these statements help you fulfill the destiny He has planned for you, you will never be all you can be and accomplish all He has for you to do. You may have a level of success, depending on how hard you work, but you will never have real significance.

That only comes through a close relationship with your King. Success is what man says about you. Significance is what God reveals to others about who you really are.

Your business should be a relational enterprise.

Leadership and ministry (your business) is about relationships. It must go beyond products, goods and services if it is to have Kingdom impact. Scripture is clear about the importance of building relationships in ever-widening circles and spheres of influence, known today as the network.

From the beginning, God created man fellowship and to be in relationship with Him and his fellow man. He called Israel out of all the nations He created to have a special relationship with Him. The calling of believers out of darkness and grafting into the family of God is for the purpose of relationship. Without real and honest relationships, few things of significant value are accomplished.

Those who serve you and your business or professional interests must feel some sort of relationship to you, if not personally, at least to your mission and vision. If not, then as a leader you have failed them. They will not be as productive as they could have been.

Relationships are not only vertical and horizontal; they should be ever widening circles. They should include family, friends, competitors and even enemies (they help keep you focused). Relationships are fundamental to life. We have them whether we want them or not.

We should always strive to make them better. Relationships provide Kingdom opportunities.

The Great Commission is about relationships. You cannot warm people to yourself, win them to Christ and develop them to be disciples without being relational. If you lead a successful and significant business, you understand the importance of relationships with your core leaders, team leaders, vendors, customers, and stakeholders.

Everything about the Kingdom is relational. Develop relationships with people, not just for business reasons but also for the purpose of winning them to Christ and helping them to be better followers—known as disciples.

Communicate the Truth as the Holy Spirit provides inspiration and direction. Teach, train, and coach new believers to deeper levels of Kingdom life and effectiveness. Equip the mature believers for the work of the church as well as church work by helping them develop their God-given gifts and talents. Finally, release the trained, equipped, and empowered to their Kingdom assignments in business, government and classrooms of higher learning – the 21st Century mission field, known as the marketplace.

Your business or professional position is your calling. Never allow yourself or others to devalue your marketplace calling. Instead, allow God to use you, your business or position to strengthen and extend his Kingdom.

Lesson 15
Leadership for the 21st century

Until the later part of the 20th Century, Fortune 500 companies' and major ministry organization's number one priority in searching for top leaders was the person's I.Q. and how productive they were. Those are still important, but the number one concern now is a person's E.Q., their emotional maturities. Their E.Q. determines how well they work with others and if they will make wise and mature decisions, especially during times of crisis and challenge.

E.Q., or emotional maturity and awareness, knows who you are in Christ and who He is in you. How you respond to others, the situations you face, and the plans you have for the future is where all leaders must begin. It is this understanding of wholeness that determines your leadership effectiveness both now and in the future. Never has the church and its leaders faced a more challenging time in a world with such an uncertain future.

Leadership has changed dramatically both in the marketplace and the church. A new set of skills and attitudes are needed in order to have impact and influence. These skills and attitudes must blend with a spiritual maturity and personal growth not demanded or even required up to this point in history.

The Church must model Luke 2:52 ("Jesus increased in wisdom and stature and favor with God and man.") if she wants to compete on the world stage at a level that will fulfill the core of the Great Commission to "disciple nations." This leadership commitment must include a deep love for the Lord and a passion to do His will without compromise.

Ministry leaders' skill sets must include an understanding and an expertise in emerging technologies and an anticipation and grasp of new opportunities. Mastering personal leadership capabilities, appreciating diversity, building partnerships and alliances, and sharing leadership roles by creating a shared vision, are all part of knowing how to lead continual change in a world that requires thinking globally.

Great leaders have more than a starting point

Achieving this level of competency requires dedication, practice, patience and the zeal of the Apostle Paul when he said *"This one thing I do..."* It also requires a starting point. Every great effort not only has a beginning, but it also has an attitude; a mindset; and a determination that things are going to change and it starts with the leader. That's what real leadership is about. It starts with your personal life; your local leadership opportunities; and your ability to see that you can make a difference...not only where you are, but globally as well.

You may not be the smartest leader, but you can be a mature leader. The Apostle Peter's final words include a warning for today's leaders during these unsettling times around the globe.

"I am warning you ahead of time, dear friends. Be on guard so you are not carried away by the errors of wicked people and lose your own secure footing. Rather, you must grow in the grace and knowledge of our Lord and Savior, Jesus Christ . . ."
—2 Peter 3:17-18 NLT

Lesson 16
Invest Your Time with Winners

Great leaders and the leadership they provide will involve a cause greater than his or her personal cause and extend beyond his or her lifetime. Sitting USA Presidents as they near the end of their influence begin talking about their legacy, what they leave behind for the generations to come. Results leaders produce good, average or poor are the foundation upon which the next generation builds.

The next generation, will they be able to build on your foundation, or will they have to lay a new one? All great leaders want to leave behind a life and ministry that gives the next generation a head start on fulfilling their own destiny. They do not need a challenge so great that it requires laying a new foundation at best or removing a lot of rubbish before they can begin at worst. See Nehemiah 4:10.

Leadership that makes a difference and outlasts your life is built on four keys. Winning and losing are not always determined by the final score but by the attitude and effort maintained during the game (your lifetime), then passed on and retained by the next generation after your game is over.

The makeup of most teams is what many call the 20-60-20 rule. In every organized effort, there are usually three groups of people. Twenty percent called Vision-Makers - top performers, sixty percent called

Vision-Supporters - average performers, and twenty percent called Vision-Drainers, less than desirable to outright negative.

Who keeps the leader up at night? Who causes most of the problems they face? You guessed it the bottom twenty percent. It always puzzles me why so many leaders spend so much time with the bottom twenty percent with so little to show for it. The reasons are many but few are justifiable. Jesus preached to the crowds, ministered wholeness too many, but spent most of his time with twelve of which eleven went on to change their world with His message of faith, hope and love.

If you are a leader (a person with influence), how should you spend your time with these three groups. Spend eighty percent of your time encouraging and enriching your Vision-Makers. Spend fifteen percent of your time training and coaching your Vision-Supporters. Spend no more than five percent of your time retraining, reassigning or releasing your Vision-Drainers.

You must move your Vision-Drainers up or out. If you do not, other team members will lose faith and respect for your leadership. If you allow them to absorb too much of your time and energy, your ability to create and sustain productive long-term results with your best people will vanish.

How do you determine who populates the 20-60-20 groups? What distinguishes a Vision-Maker, Vision-Supporter and Vision-Drainer? I use the following seven performance areas to help make that determination. In a scale of 1-5, where do your team members rank in possessing the following traits?

Spirit of Excellence.
Spirit of Faith.
Spirit of Competence.
Spirit of Commitment.
Spirit of Awareness.
Spirit of Love.
Spirit of Teamwork.

You can teach solid principles but the *spirit of something* is caught more than taught. You must model the spirit of these if your teaching of the principles is effective.

How do you handle your 20-60-20 team members on a daily basis? Your **Vision-Makers** create solutions when problems arise in pursuit of the vision. Do not abuse or take them for granted. Your **Vision-Supporters** can identify problems but may lack knowledge or sufficient experience to find a solution. They need adequate teaching, training and superior coaching coupled with significant learning opportunities. Your **Vision-Drainers** identify problems that have no solutions and blame others for their inadequate or poor performance.

Before you move them up or out, try the following. Describe what you have observed in their behavior. Be fair, firm and honest. Evaluate how you feel about their performance without being judgmental and share openly with them one on one. Show what needs to change or improve.

Be clear about what are acceptable standards and performance expectations. Give additional teaching and training if necessary. Remember, no amount of teaching or training will make up for a poor attitude or non-productive work ethic. Trying to coach either or both is frustrating.

Make sure they understand the consequences of continued poor performance and give them a definite time line for improvement. Have them summarize your conversation and commit to making needed changes.

No leader I know is blessed with all Vision-Makers on their leadership journey. Even Jesus did not have all *winners*. On many occasion he picked people that others ignored and turned them into champions. A great example is David the shepherd boy who became a giant killer and eventually the greatest earthly king (Leader) upon whose throne the King of Kings will sit.

Great leaders know how to identify and work with all three groups but spend the majority of their time with Vision-Makers. If you want your leadership to make a difference during your lifetime and go beyond, you must do the same.

Lesson 17
Great Leaders Build Strong Foundations

Leaders who make a difference during their lifetime and develop a ministry that lasts beyond their lifetime must lay a strong foundation. The *upper room experience* became a marketplace reality because a foundation was laid that has stood the test of time for more than 2000 years.

This kind of foundation is built with purpose, passion and sustainable results. These core values must govern and reinforce your mission, vision and long-term goals, but your decisions and daily actions of every team member.

Leaders must develop a ministry culture that esteems and relentlessly practices these core values and behaviors if they want a spirit of excellence and sustainable results to prevail.

How do you create and sustain the kind of ministry culture that develops a ministry of significance makes a difference in your generation and lays a solid foundation for the next one?

Build your foundation on the following ten principles

A spirit of love demonstrated at all times by loving, accepting and forgiving everyone who gets involved with your ministry. I Corinthians 13; I John

A spirit of faith demonstrated by the attitude we convey, the words we speak and don't speak, and the actions we display. Faith only works in an atmosphere of love. We are overcomers through Christ, and we will act as such. —2 Corinthians 4

A spirit of excellence surrounds every aspect of our ministry whether it is in the church or the marketplace. Excellence is not a goal to reach for but a way of life to live. Excellence is an inner passion to please Christ in everything we do not perfectionism, an outward struggle to please the expectations of others. —Mark 7:37

Everyone on your team is passionate about discovering, developing and deploying the next generation of leaders, not just improving the skills of current leaders for today's challenges. —Mark 3:13-15

You build your ministry culture around servant-leadership at all levels. Senior leaders lead by influence and not by title, position or power. They lead by example and not by commands and directives. If your influence and example does not get it done little else, you do matters. —Mark 10:45

Align behaviors, actions and processes with goals and values. Reward the results you want and you will get more out of what you want. Check out the Constitution of the Kingdom in Mathew 7.

You measure and evaluate the important things - not just the urgent things. Important things are seldom urgent and urgent things are seldom important. Great leaders rarely stray from their core values in the pursuit of their vision. —Matthew 25

You create ownership through individual and team accountability. You rarely get true accountability when you demand it. It works best when offered freely. That means you get vital information before you ask for it. —Matthew 24:45-47

Recognize and reward both small and big *wins*. Individuals and teams can never have too many wins. You may not come in first in every race but you can finish every race and that makes you a winner. Napoleon said he won the battle for Europe by passing out ribbons. Read Numbers 18:31; I Timothy 5:18; Revelation 22:12.

Practice saturation communication at all levels. You can give too much information at times but you can never communicate too much. Remember, telling is not always teaching, and listening is not always learning. Using Email, Facebook and Twitter is not communicating only giving information.

Read Galatians 6:6; Matthew 5:37; I Timothy 6:18; Hebrews 13:16.

These ten principles are the building blocks for the foundation of great leadership. Leadership that lasts beyond your lifetime cannot be laid on a weak foundation. It may take longer in the beginning but resist the temptation to cut corners here. If you do, you put your entire leadership future in jeopardy. Many high profile leaders have crashed and burned because of a poor foundation.

Lesson 18

Great leaders create a path for leadership excellence

If you want to move forward, go to the next level, develop a spirit of excellence, see consistent and sustainable results at all levels you must develop leadership competency and consistency at all levels.

Most of the available resources are invested in those at the senior level and very little given to those who most of the time need it the most—entry-level leaders. You must take the same care and concern in the development of your leaders at this level as you do the development of your budgets and strategic planning.

What we tolerate, we will not change. What we permit is what we promote. Every organization must constantly ask, *"What is keeping us from going to the next level and seeing our vision be a reality?"* What is stopping you? What will it take your organization to make a difference in your generation and lay a solid foundation for the one to follow?

Be brutally honest with yourself and your core leaders by defining what is standing in our way to victory. Remember, leadership inconsistencies at any level make it difficult to accomplish the following three things:

1. Achieve overall organizational goals.
2. Develop a culture of love, faith and excellence.

3. Bring satisfaction to all team members and stakeholders.

You may state them differently in the church world vs. the marketplace but the issues remain the same. Do not allow leadership inconsistencies to remain very long. Any single leader's autonomy is less important than the organization's mission and vision regardless of their status, position or longevity. People and issues seldom get better with age without some significant intervention.

How do you create a path for leadership excellence?

Here are seven steps that have helped me through the years:

Make sure all leaders are using a common agenda as it relates to defining present reality and the future. First, this aligns all Team Members and connects everyone on a regular basis to your mission, vision, values and strategy. Second, it provides a single tool for communicating so everyone understands and commits to factors critical for success individually, as a team and the overall effort.

Align whatever measurement and evaluation tools you use to your values and goals. Never forget, you plant the seeds of your vision in the soil known as values. Conflicting values create 90% of the battles in most organizations.

Goals are more than good ideas, wishes, desires or hopes. There is a seven-step process for setting legitimate goals. Most of all focus your goals on sustainable results not just activity.

Make sure every team leader has accurate and adequate information to share with their team. The information should be relevant, show a direct connection to the vision, and how teams relate to each other. It is the only way for team leaders to make informed decisions and keep their teams inspired. Have a clear and concise action plan for how future leaders at all levels is recruited, developed, deployed, coached and evaluated.

Have clarity about how *tough questions* are solicited, evaluated and responses given. Help your leaders develop skills necessary to address these questions in a positive way that reflects well on your organization. This builds confidence in them, their team and all stakeholders.

Train all leaders for competency in the "Five Things Every Leader Needs to Know" regardless of where their efforts take place—in the church or the marketplace.

1. You need to know your God.
2. You need to know Yourself.
3. You need to know your Brother.
4. You need to know your Ministry.
5. You need to know your Mission.

If you don't train your leaders in these five areas, you can be sure someone else will. Current technology and the social media have done as much to confuse your leaders, as it has to help them, if not more. Make sure you know where they are in these areas.

Above all else—leaders and the leadership they provide must be consistent and competent if above average sustainable results happen on a regular basis. Examples:

Airline Pilots—Have a pre-flight, in-flight and post-flight checklist. I certainly did not want them experimenting during my recent 15 hour flight to South Africa.

Restaurants—McDonald's, Cracker Barrel or Ruth Chris want the food to look good, presented well and taste the same no matter where you experience their service. Consistency always builds confidence.

Medical Staff—Doctors spend years learning, practicing and perfecting their skills. We do not want them experimenting with some new technique when we are lying on the table.

As leaders, we should be no less diligent in creating a path for leadership excellence in our organization or ministry effort.

Lesson 19
Leadership's top ten

You must believe your leadership makes a difference.

Everyone makes a difference. The only question is what kind and how much. If you do not believe what you do matters, then it usually does not. Visionary leadership is about making changes that matter and make a difference. If nothing changes you are not leading - you are managing.

The leader who has the most influence is the one who creates significant, substantial and sustainable change. Without change, there is no difference. Your leadership matters only if there is a positive difference after you move on.

Others must believe in you.

If people do not believe in you, they will not believe your message, regardless if the message is true or valuable. If they do not follow you willingly, they will not follow you closely, for very long or very far. Charisma and compensation may attract people, but only relational equity, built on the fulfillment of the following expectations keeps them following:

Integrity—you tell the truth all the time and maintain a strong, ethical behavior in every situation. You follow through on your promises.

Vision—you create and lead a shared vision with clarity and passion, not fulfilling your personal ambitions.

Inspiration—you know the difference between inspiration and motivation. You are a hope dealer for tomorrow not a dream killer today.

Competence—you know what you are talking about and can do it, not just talk about it. You have the leadership skills for developing people and building teams that fulfill the vision.

Your values are clear, simple and meaningful

Values are the soil in which the seeds of your vision are planted, nurtured and matured. You gain buy-in and commitment by everyone through agreement on team values. You never commit to anything unless you see the value. If personal values conflict with the team's values, you become an actor and no longer a player.

Your title, office and position are not who you are, values are who you are. Values create the environment in which you give leadership. Conflicting values create most problems in any relationship.

Your vision distinguishes your leadership

Your ability to create, define and communicate the vision is what makes you a visionary leader. If you spend more than 30% of your time looking through the microscope at the present, you are not a leader who creates the future but a manager of the present.

If, you focus more on what could be rather than what is, you are a leader. If you focus on what is you produce more of what is. If you focus on what could be you produce more of what could be.

Vision provides meaning to what you do every day. If what you do does not move you closer to vision fulfillment, why do it?

You are a team builder and not a team user

Jesus was the best. Follow his model of the Twelve and the Seventy spoken about in Matthew 10. Visionary leadership is not selfish or done in isolation. Your ability to build teams determines the width and depth of your influence and success. If you can't build a team, find one to join.

Building great teams through relational equity and vision is not accomplished through inspirational speaking but passionate listening. You must understand hearts and minds if you keep hands and feet for the long haul and during tough times. Tone-deaf leaders create negative emotions, confusion, and eventually discord and strife.

Your team members must feel capable, confident, and empowered. Ask questions, listen to your heart, provide support, develop skills, create agreement, stay aligned and above all – make emotional connections.

Create, develop, and strengthen
accountability through trust

Trust is the glue and lubricant of every organization. To gain trust, you must be trust worthy. You have to be worthy of trust and reliable. You must give trust before receiving trust. Trust is your license for giving leadership. If you lose your *Trust License,* it is extremely difficult to get it back. In most cases, you never regain the same level of trust while leading the same team.

If you want to be trusted, you have to be vulnerable. Your values must be clear, your expectations understood, predictable, consistent, candid and forthright. You can have trust without accountability but you cannot have accountability without trust.

How you handle challenges reveals your character, develops your leadership skills and determines your impact

All significant accomplishments involve adversity, change and challenges because all great leaders are not the product of an easy road or protected environment. You always learn more from your failures than your successes.

You must learn how to overcome—not just avoid the tough times. Wisdom will help you avoid many things but not all things. Setbacks and adversity make some of life's best teachers. Use them to your advantage and never as a gage of success or failure.

Model the behavior you desire in others.

Base your behavior on your values or you forfeit your leadership influence even if you do not lose your position. Your greatest leadership influence is the model you live not the position you hold or the title you carry. Your greatest leadership strength should be the example you set. DWYSYWD!

Your actions must be consistent with your articulation. What you say may be interesting, thoughtful or even inspiring but what you do is what your team will do.

Admit your mistakes and move on. Make restitution if necessary - it builds confidence and earns trust. Your words and actions are audible and visible reminders to your team of what is and is not important.

Maintain a learning curve

Learning must remain a core value. When you stop learning, you stop growing and death sets in. When you think you know it all - look again - you may have missed something. What you learn after you know it all separates great leaders from average and good leaders.

Learning is a passionate pursuit not a goal to accomplish. It takes time, effort and focus. Genius is not the quantity of what you know, but the revelation there is more to learn. It requires a strategy for growth that includes goals and objectives. Re-train, re-assign or replace leaders who stop growing in leadership skills and knowledge.

Lead from the heart – not just the head.

You must love what you do and show it to those who help you do it. You show you care by paying attention, making people feel important, and empowering your team for their destiny.

Leaders should not ignore the emotional element vital in energizing individuals and teams. Challenges engage the hands, vision engages the feet, logic engages the mind, but only love and passion engage the heart.

One of life's tragedies is seeing a challenge and thinking it is someone else's responsibility. A greater tragedy is thinking every challenge is your personal responsibility. Great leadership is accepting only the challenges God has called and gifted you to solve.

At the end of your leadership journey you will be remembered for two things—the problems you solved and the problems you created. May God give you the wisdom and skill to solve more problems than you create.

Lesson 20

Lead according to the times—not according to tradition

"The sons of Issachar, men who understood the times, with knowledge of what Israel should do"
—I Chronicles 12.

All the men listed in this chapter came in full battle array to Hebron with the single purpose of making David the king of Israel, but it seems only the men of Issachar knew what to do.

Our nation is facing many challenges but without Divine intervention, there seems to be no answers. Issachar and his 200 men faced a challenging moment in the life of Israel and God gave them divine revelation of what to do. May He do the same with the leaders of our nation as they face challenges never seen before in our nation, and a world that is smaller and more complex every day.

More important than who is president of the USA, is how effective are Christian leaders where God has assigned them? What is the biggest factor in the ability of a ministry or organization to have long-term influence, impact and success in fulfilling its mission?

It is not an outstanding mission, vision or value statements important as those are. Not the latest information and communication technologies as vital as those are in the 21st Century. Not even access to unlimited ministry tools, time, and money as helpful as they would be.

I believe most important is the ability to hear the voice of the Spirit, follow His strategy, develop the passion to innovate, and adapt as He leads us during these very challenging times. There must be sensitivity for his voice, not only for our nation, but for the Church and marketplace as well.

Could it be, while most in the Church have maintained a strong allegiance to the Inerrant Word of God (the map), we have lost our sensitivity to the compass (the Holy Spirit) while endeavoring to follow the map?

If you are going to maximize the opportunities the Church has today in the marketplace, you need to develop and mobilize leaders at all levels of ability, talent and gifting. They must *understand the times and know what to do.* All leaders need to be functioning effectively at every level of leadership, every opportunity and challenge in the church and in the marketplace.

If you are going to lead according to the times and not tradition, you must have the courage to invest all available resources; money, good will, energy, facilities and ministry tools in new and innovative ways without abandoning the best of yesterday. Believing you can carry all the baggage of yesterday into the tomorrow's God has planned is naive. Wise and courageous leaders know the difference, as did the men of Issachar.

Four vital things that today's "Men of Issachar" must understand and execute:

First—knowing the difference between leading and managing your ministry or marketplace effort; setting goals for your innovative ideas and understanding today's and tomorrow's leadership/management realities.

Second—managers are doers and leaders are visionaries. Both are vital for success. Managers are about efficiency, procedures and coordinating the bureaucracy. They keep us on the right path today but provide little, if any, direction for the future. They tend to limit imagination, creativity and slow progress or change. However, today would not happen without them.

Leaders are visionaries. They dream about how the future can be.

"...behold the dreamer cometh...let us kill him...and we shall see what will become of his dreams."—Genesis 37:19-20.

Be careful whom you share your dream with but have one. If you do not you should be managing and allow someone else to lead with their dream.

Visionary leaders should allow two things guide their envisioning process —innovation and inspiration. Innovation is based on wisdom, knowledge and understanding inspired by the Holy

Spirit. It is causing resources and influence flow to those who add value and away from those who do not.

Inspiration is a sense of mission, vision and passion for living for a cause greater than you are. Innovation and inspiration always increase stakeholder value. Just as today's success won't happen without great managers, tomorrow's vision won't happen without great leaders.

Third—when talking about innovative goals for ministry in the church and marketplace consider at least three:

Great leaders always foster ministry and organizational renewal. Too many wait until conditions demand that something be done. Smart leaders are always considering how we do what we do and how to do it better.

Great leaders make significant changes before they have to. Good leaders make changes when they have to and poor leaders resist change and try to make changes when they are no longer necessary or will not have any significant impact on the future.

Great leaders constantly inspire their team to make innovation everyone's passion. They are in a constant state of war against the status quo. Challenging the process is not an occasional event but a way of life. Innovation is valued and embraced by every leader at every level, not resisted

Great leaders continually cultivate and develop creativity

"So it is with effective leadership. The leader whose thinking is constrained within well-worn ruts; who is completely governed by his established passions and prejudices; who is incapable of thinking either grey or free; and who can't even appropriate the creative imagination and fresh ideas of those around him is as anachronistic and ineffective as the dinosaur.

He may by dint of circumstances, remain in power but his followers would almost certainly be better off without him."
Dr. Steven Sample, President USC

The two biggest traditional threats to this kind of creative and innovative environment are, *"We've never done it that way before."* A close second is *"What's in it for me?"* Great leaders constantly and firmly resist these traditions and insist their team members do the same.

Fourth—leaders who *lead according to the times and know what to do*; understand today and tomorrow's leadership and management realities.

They understand that information and communication technologies are a lot like the internet. They are available to just about anyone in the world. They are transparent, have few if any secrets. They are reliant on personal integrity; a lot of personal financial gain is at stake and tremendous peer pressure to stay connected. Leaders who don't understand this reality find their ability to lead effectively greatly challenged.

Understanding our times and helping those we lead know what to do should be at the top of every leader's prayer list and active agenda. We must get them ready for eternity, but also ready for tomorrow. The world is trying to help people cope with today's challenges. Dr. Phil, Oprah, and many others seem to have the answers but we know better. God help us as leaders, not only help our people cope; but lead them on a mission to be *more than conquerors through Jesus Christ our Lord*; in the home, the church and the marketplace.

The greatest challenge for those who choose to lead according to the times and not tradition, is constantly enlarging our thinking, while being led of the Spirit to respond with courage and conviction to the best ideas not every idea. The Sons of Issachar did, Jesus did, why not you?

Lesson 21

Titles and positions don't make a leader

Give some people a title or a position and it seems to ruin their ability to serve or lead. Titles and positions do not make a leader. They may affirm and define the person called leader, but they never determine the person's success. Values cultivation is always more important than metrics, skill, or performing the latest best practice.

Leadership influence and position gained by nepotism or tenure is seldom as good as that gained through experience and significant learning opportunities over time. Productive leadership influence always balances personal gain with social and responsible resource investment unless you have experience and are exposed to learning opportunities, nothing but personal ambition is gained, while much is lost by shortcutting the process.

Lessons are learned with every leadership opportunity at every level. Too many want the title or position of authority but are unwilling to pay the price while maintaining a spirit of humility through the process. Too many want the fruit but do not want to climb the tree. Fruit that falls at your feet is usually rotten and passed over by the real tree climbers. It is the same with leadership. If you get your position, any other way than climbing to the top through blood, sweat and tears it shows up soon and in so many ways.

Leadership is 20% tools, methods, systems, skill, and 80% emotional maturity. Emotional maturity can be defined as productive behavior on a consistent basis. It is not so much what you say, but how you say it, and how you behave when saying it. In productive organizations, leaders have mature conversations across all levels of the talent pool.

These conversations should be designed to engage, inspire, educate, and develop present and potential leaders at all levels. People are not looking for a title or position to lean on but a leader to follow, regardless of title or position.

Smart must be a verb, not just a noun. Intellectual genius is good, but knowing what to do with it is even better. However, having accurate and adequate information, building teams with winning attitudes, and knowing how to execute a relevant strategy is the best. Great leadership used to be defined by how well you handled a challenge or crisis. Now it is about how soon you anticipate and prepare for one.

When a crisis or challenge comes, you had better have more than a title or position. Titles and positions engraved on custom-made business cards and framed certificates covering your office wall have little to do with any of these things.

Organizations who want to influence the marketplace, for whatever reason, need leaders who are emotionally mature, culturally relevant, and smart—as in a verb, not a noun. If titles and positions do not make good followers, why do we think they make good leaders? True servant-leaders never need a title or a position to make a difference.

How do you know if you have a servant's heart? Watch how you respond when you are treated like one. Take all the titles away, all the signs down indicating rank or order, and within 30 days or less, strangers will know the real leaders.

Lesson 22
Performance Expectation Management

"The best job description in the world never guarantees superior job performance, good job performance, or even adequate job performance. At best, it gives a general overview and functional expectations; at worst, it can be detrimental to job performance if not done properly."

Three Terms Leaders of Leaders Need to Understand and Use Consistently

First, there is the *Performance Agreement*. This is what the performance looks like and vital in finding agreement on what a win (success) looks like. You design performance agreements to communicate the *big picture*. They are not performance contract that determine continued employment or status on the team. Accountability stands a better chance of succeeding if everyone on the Team embraces responsibility for his or her own *performance* and the larger responsibility for the their team and organization's success.

Spend time with individual team members explaining how their *performance* affects the mission and vision of the overall effort. This communication helps team members understand and make wiser decisions from the context of the *big picture* rather than the perspective of what seems as a detailed and insignificant task.

State your clear and concise expectations of their performance. If you are vague in any critical area, it is bound to show up later. Solving these questions sooner is always better than later. If one person on the Team does not meet the expectations of their Performance Agreement at best, it is disappointing and at worst, it affects the Team's performance and causes failure, disappointment and if not corrected, bitterness and resentment.

It is important from the beginning you state clearly and concisely Performance expectations. There must be agreement and alignment behind these expectations. They should be clearly written and repeated often until everyone *gets it*. It is hard to proactive and aggressive if you are confused about what is expected. You avoid most of the frustrations between leaders and team members, especially new hires, with a good performance agreement at the beginning.

The Performance Agreement should include, but not limited to dates, time sensitive issues, goals and vision. Define their responsibilities' and to whom are they accountable? Include major components of all tasks they perform and how you expect the finished effort delivered quality and quantity. *If your expectations are fuzzy or confusing in any way, disappointment sets in, teamwork suffers and many times important details fall through the cracks.*

For accountability and responsibility to work there must be consequences for failure following through with Performance Agreements.

Without consequences, team members will not take them seriously and very little changes. If individuals and teams deliver superior ministry effort, they need adequate, prompt and regular recognition and rewards.

Second, is the periodic *Performance Review*. Do a periodic review of the team member's performance. Are we on target? If not, what adjustments need made to fine-tune the Agreement? Poorly designed or communicated performance agreements always require major adjustments.

The following six questions will help these periodic reviews and well worth the time, effort and resources.

Six-Questions that Help Managers become Better Coaches

The manager has a one-on-one dialogue with each direct report for about 60 minutes every three months. The "rules" are very simple. Ask both parties to: Come prepared with the questions filled out make each question a dialogue, not dictate

Listen to the other person's ideas and try to implement what you can

Try not to "prove" the other person is wrong and at the end, consolidate the notes.

Where is the organization going?

The manager outlines where the organization is going in terms of vision, goals and priorities.

Where are you and your team going?

The manager asks the teammate where their team is going in terms of supporting the vision, goals and priorities of the manager. The manager provides feedback on where the team should be going and solidifies priorities. By involving teammates in this ongoing dialogue, managers build alignment and commitment to the organization's vision.

What is going well with you and your team?

The manager highlights the accomplishments the teammate and their team have performed since the last time they met. The manager also notes the strengths of the teammate in terms of both being consistent to the core values as well as performance. The manager then asks, "Did I forget anything you and your team have done well?"

The manager learns "good news" that may have otherwise been missed which ensures they recognize achievement and understand positive performance so the teammate feels appreciated.

What are the opportunities to improve for you and your team?

Mangers ask the teammate what are the opportunities for you and your team to improve. Then the manager adds or modifies the list of improvements for the teammate. Also includes professional development plan.

How can the manager help?

Managers listen to their teammate's suggestions on how they can become more helpful. They can also suggest approaches and then ask, "Do you feel this approach will help you become more effective?"

Where can the manager improve?

Managers that ask teammates how they can improve in one or two key behaviors and follow-ups on a quarterly basis are seen as dramatically increasing leadership effectiveness. Asking for feedback changes the dynamics of the coaching process. Traditional coaching is usually thought of as a one-way monologue that focuses on, "Let me tell you what you can do to improve."

Creating a two-way dialogue that focuses on helping each other, makes teammates more willing for coaching since managers are willing to be coached!

Third, is the *Performance Management* process that uses a good Performance Agreement and a strong partnership in the Performance Review producing superior performance.

Why Continual Clarification is Important

There must be continual clarification around the purpose of all three terms. The number one reason is moving the team from disagreement and/or lack of understanding to full *agreement*. The number two reason is when moving the team from *agreement* to *alignment* of individual performance with Team performance.

This movement is the only thing that produces momentum and leads to *allegiance* (commitment to mission and vision—not personalities) and long-term commitment.

Make sure you align individual performance and team performance with the organization's Mission, Values, Vision,and stated Goals & Objectives.

Values documentation, if your values are not stated publically and modeled by core leaders consistently any statement you have is useless. Modeling core values should be part of any performance agreement and review.

Documentation helps identify, clarify and make needed adjustments in the areas of learning, growth, training and coaching.

Job descriptions (alone) at best cannot identify much less make-needed improvement in vital areas that deliver superior job performance. You must have a performance agreements and reviews for sustainable improvement. Both must be clear, concise and current to have any value.

Leading Others to Reach Their Full Potential

On-going feedback and dialogue both aid in clarifying and understanding performance expectations. To be sure, performance expectations measured against mission, vision, values and stated goals always lead to maximum potential. Be clear about how they do. Clarity about individual and Team performance contributes to achieving organizational and leadership strategies.

Clear Performance Agreements along with strong partnership in Performance Reviews and a simple yet comprehensive Performance Management process, will provide reward and motivation for giving extra effort in challenging opportunities and situations.

Lesson 23
Prepare, empower and entrust the next generation

Preparing, empowering and entrusting the next generation when their time has come are a constant challenge for current generations. Saul won his thousand but David won his ten thousand. This created an opportunity for rejoicing or jealousy. Leadership is not about titles, position and perks, but influence and commitment to the next generation.

If we served our generation well our "sons and daughters" should be doing more, doing it better and with greater results. Every leadership transition and generational shift should leverage the next generation of leaders. We should hand them the baton willingly, step aside with grace and leave an open track for them to run on.

"My son heard me say, entrust reliable men to be able to teach others also." —2 Timothy 2:1-2

Great leaders are always planting trees under which they will never enjoy the shade, building fires that will never warm them and creating resources they will never invest. This kind of foresight always separates great leaders from average or poor.

"You have many instructors but few fathers." —I Corinthians 4:15

Abraham said in Hebrews 11:11 that he was enabled to become a father because his faith rested in the one who made the promise. Fathering must be more than a mark of physical and intellectual maturity. It should also signify spiritual and emotional maturity. Passing on what we have learned to the next generation through the power of the Holy Spirit should be the high water mark of our maturity and servant-leadership.

Do it while you still live and you have the joy of seeing it happen. Wait until your life on earth is over and you pass on with only the hope that it might happen. If you do the latter, you fail in preparing and empowering the next generation and possibly leave a foundation that must be rebuilt.

Apostle Paul says in I Corinthians 15, *"therefore I urge you to imitate me."* You can learn most everything you need to know by following, watching and listening. But, you must exchange seats if you want to learn how and be competent. There is a significant difference between knowing and doing.

Universities, colleges and other learning institutions must not confuse instruction with on-the-job training. You never develop competency and confidence in classrooms, only on the front lines through significant learning opportunities. Books, seminars, and consultants will never replace seasoned spiritual warriors who are now energized fathers, mentors and coaches.

As mentors and coaches, we must not leave the car or the playing field. We must continue to ride, put our life and all that we have built to this point, and entrust it to the next generation of leaders. We must never forget that we teach to know, train for competence and coach for excellence. Seldom does one person do all three and rarely at the same time.

Elisha asked Elijah for a double portion. Herein lays the challenge for presiding leaders. Do you want the next generation to be almost as good, just as good or far better? Every current leadership team makes this choice, either on purpose or by default. Best choices are seldom by accident or left to chance.

You evidence real maturity in by preparing, empowering and releasing – not holding back or holding on. Mature leaders never create a container for the next generation to keep full. They hand over a clean slate upon which the next generation determines their own vision of the original purpose. No generation should see themselves as creators of a final solution but creators of new opportunities for the next generation to exploit and then become their greatest cheerleaders.

Too many wait until they are a part of the *"great cloud of witnesses"* mentioned in Hebrews 12 before they cheer. Mature leaders never wait too long before giving their successors the liberty to fly away from the nest they created – even if they go in a direction they would not have chosen. Concerns about the next generation straying from the original purpose should be addressed long before it's time to step aside. You win those battles best during a sufficient time of transition, not on the day; you transfer leadership to the next generation.

Every generation is important, but for different reasons. Infants (new members) indicate new life and hope for the future. Children are sponges for knowledge and grow quickly. Adolescents are determined to break the mold and create their own path. Young adults (20-45) are the key to any successful generational shift and leadership transition. Elders (50+) are gold mines of wisdom and experience. They are a blessing to every generation.

The 20-45 year old generation must own the vision but not necessarily the resources. With privileges come responsibilities. With responsibilities comes influence. With influence come partnerships. With partnerships comes wisdom. With wisdom comes ownership. There is no handbook that defines how a particular generation must live the journey of generational and leadership transition. But, if there is not a clear and smooth transition to the next generation, done in a timely manner, future success is doubtful at best and certain failure at worst.

Great leaders move over when they don't have too but sense the time is right. Good leaders move over when the handwriting is on the wall. Poor leaders seldom have a sense of timing and present reality. They usually ignore the handwriting on the wall until surrendering the reigns of leadership making very little difference for the next generation. By this time significant momentum has been lost, damage is occurring rapidly, and decay has set in.

Leaders over fifty have the greatest opportunity to prepare, empower and entrust the next generation if they will leverage their leadership through the next generation sooner rather than later. May God help all leadership teams know when this *kairos* moment arrives. It is not so much about a date on the calendar but a revelation by the Holy Spirit that both generations understand, prepare for, and execute when the time is right.

Lesson 24
Prophetic Impact in the Marketplace

Marketplace ministers (Ephesians 4:1) have made a substantial difference for decades with little or no affirmation from the accepted, traditional or five-fold gift ministers (Ephesians 4:11).

I believe the cause has been more a lack of understanding or misunderstanding than intentional. There are exceptions but not enough, given the challenge in the marketplace harvest field that generates and controls the world economy, governments and educational institutions.

Marketplace ministers are not agents or representatives of the five-fold gift ministers, just the opposite. Prophetic impact in the marketplace requires understanding and partnership on the part of both groups of ministers. Each has a vital role to play. The command in Matthew 28 goes unanswered without the synergy created when both groups understand their own call and role along with the others.

It's time the Church, via marketplace ministers, steps up and provides "thus says the Lord" prophetic impact. I have seen evidence in the marketplace of all the Ephesians 4 ascension gifts in my 45 years of marketplace experience. There are leaders who have an apostolic gift; others have prophetic, pastor, teacher or evangelist. The fear of titles and offices has greatly weakened or sometimes eliminated the effects of these gifts in the marketplace.

The Church can have more impact scattered than it does gathered if she understands her Kingdom mandate. We must never abandon the exhortation to *"not forsake the assembling of ourselves together,"* but remember all the reasons for that gathering. One is equipping the saints (Ephesians 4:1 ministers) for the work of the ministry that has direct connection to the (Kingdom) marketplace.

Prophetic impact goes beyond providing informational teaching. There must be a prophetic declaration that redeems, transforms and brings people into a life-changing relationship with their Creator. Prophetic declaration creates and maintains a sense of urgency for extending the Kingdom – not swelling the membership roles and attendance figures of local congregations.

Prophetic impact involves marketplace ministers who live and share the gospel "as one having authority and not as the scribes." (Mark 1:22) Prophetic declarations challenge and echo freedom for the masses held in bondage because of satanic deception. It provides Divine strategies for moving people from despair and hopelessness to a life filled with hope, peace and true joy.

Marketplace ministers are hope-dealers

Prophetic gifted marketplace ministers are hope-dealers not purveyors of gloom and doom. It's the message of hope Jesus came preaching that produced true repentance and transformed lives. At the same time, prophetic declaration does not ignore sin and all its forms of evil that have invaded every segment of the marketplace. There must be no compromise or lack of clarity in our declaration of the Kingdom message. There should be no untouchable issue regardless of the cost.

2 Timothy 2:15 must be the foundation for all marketplace ministers. "Be diligent to present yourself to God, a worker who does not need to be afraid (or ashamed), rightly dividing the Word of Truth." (NKLV) The Greek word *spovdazo* (diligent) is also translated *study*. It means, "Be very active," implying intimate acquaintance with the Author that provides mature understanding and revelation.

If we have, "*been given all authority in heaven and earth*" (Matthew 28:18), we must give diligent preparation for that role. Many have significant opportunities only to fail and "...turn back in the day of battle." Too many high-profile ministers, in both groups of ministers, were given a world platform only to compromise and fail to give a prophetic declaration in the name of political correctness. Jesus said the Gospel would be an offense but the messenger should not be offensive, i.e., Jonah. Nonetheless, it must be delivered if we are to have prophetic impact.

John the Baptist confronted the evil and religious spirits of his day. He called people to repentance and holiness. His life was such an example many confused him with the Messiah to come. His message had credibility because of the life he lived. Can we do or be any less in our generation and marketplace opportunities?

The price for prophetic impact in the marketplace

There is a price to pay for prophetic impact. When we confront the cultural evils of our day, there is always a cost. Many who spoke up for God in Hebrews 11 ended up being stoned, imprisoned, mocked, tortured and crucified? It's happening now to our brothers and sisters in restricted nations.

How many, especially in the West, are willing to be blessed according to Matthew 5:11-12 "...bless them which persecute you, revile you and say all manner of evil against you falsely for my sake? Yes, the cost for prophetic impact is great, but the payoff far greater. Let's not be *"idle at the 11th hour in the marketplace."*

Lesson 25
Seven passions of great leaders

Passion usually implies strong emotions that tend to have an overpowering or compelling effect. Great leaders are anything, but passionless. If you are going to lead people to accomplish anything of significant value, passion is involved. If not, few follow because climb is usually higher, and the challenges are greater. The longer the journey requires leaders' who are not only convinced their cause is just, have made up minds and the passion to win burns hot.

Leaders are passionate about many things. Here is the great leadership top seven, not necessarily in ranking order or standing alone, but as a group working in harmony regardless of effort.

1
They have a passion for gaining Truth and the knowledge

All progress is the result of making wise choices. Proverbs 19:2 says the key to possessing wisdom is rooted in the habit of staying on a learning curve for life. *"My people perish for a lack of knowledge."* Great leadership begins with an awareness of the facts and a large range of information. But, it goes far beyond that in a pursuit of the Truth. Facts will help you deal clearly with present reality but only a revelation of the Truth prepares you for an unknown future.

2
They have a passion for possessing excellence in wisdom

Discipline is the result of knowing the facts and acting on them. Excellence comes over time as you become intimate with the Truth. Wisdom is knowledge put into proper actions. At the heart of wisdom is a life-long commitment to excellence. Excellence is not a goal to reach for but a way of life built on God-honoring standards and principles learned only by a passion for wisdom. Excellence will propel you to new and higher levels of performance.

3
They have a passion for discernment and discretion

Decisions based on wise discernment and discretion determines your future. Discernment and discretion are wisdom in action. Great leaders make decisions every day that affect their health, finances, family, and emotional and spiritual well-being. These affect not only his or her lives but also usually the lives of many others.

I Corinthians 10:13 says, *"But remember that the temptations that come into your life are no different from what others experience. And, God is faithful. He will keep the temptation from becoming so strong that you can't stand up against it. When you are so tempted, He will show you a way out so that you will not give in to it."* (NLT) Make right choices—blessings in your future depends on it.

4
They have a passion for honesty and integrity.

In today's culture, we don't lie anymore, *we miss-speak.* Finding a leader today who tells the truth (honesty) and one who tells the truth all the time (integrity), is challenging to say the least. *"People who wink at wrong cause trouble but a bold reproof promotes peace. The words of the godly lead to life; evil people cover up their harmful intentions."* —Proverbs 10:9-11. (NLT)

5
They have a passion for humility

The balance for strength in leadership and humbleness in attitude is a constant battle for most leaders. A lifestyle of humility leads to the discovery and admission of your *shortcomings* (momentary failures) and *weaknesses* (areas in you and your leadership in which God has not gifted you and you will never be strong.)

Pretending to be either strong or humble will not fill the gaps in your life or leadership. Only awareness plus action, based on humility will close the gap. Proverbs 22:4 says, "True humility and fear of the Lord lead to honor, riches, and long life." (NLT) Only ruthlessly ridding ourselves of false pride and false humility leads to a life of having more than we need the respect of our peers and a life worth living.

6
They have a passion for Spirit-led discipline and surrender.

We often hear about self-discipline but many times this leads to self-destruction and dozens of personality disorders so prevalent today. Proverbs 15:32, talks about a person who neglects himself ends up despising himself. Despise means to live below your dignity, to down yourself with contempt and living without discipline. This leads to a lack of confidence at best and a poor self-image at worst. Now the cover-up begins and many times addictions take over. *"The complacency of fools will destroy them."*

Discipline and surrender for Christian leaders should not be a work of the flesh and assigned totally to the will of man. Yes, it is tough work disciplining yourself but if you don't, the text says you walk on to the destruction of complacency. But as you have a revelation of who you are in Christ and Who He is in you—he Holy Spirit will guide you a long this most difficult path. He will take you from being self-disciplined (which is good) to being Spirit-disciplined, which is far better. The former is a battle from without while the latter is an internal surrender producing satisfying results.

7
They have a passion to live within limits

In every area of life, health, finances and relationships great leaders understand the value and necessity of limits. Learning to live within your limits while serving an unlimited God separates good leaders from great leaders. Most people and too many leaders live on the launching pad of life never rising to their full potential. Why, because they ignore or refuse to follow the limits of a Biblical lifestyle.

I Corinthians 9:27, talks about beating your body daily and bringing it into subjection. Philippians exhorts us to have the mind of Christ. I Corinthians 13 give us great wisdom on loving relationships. Malachi 3 provides the secret to handling your finances.

We should never limit God in any circumstance. Great leaders know their own limits and boundaries and should know them for those they lead.

Lesson 26

Create leaders everywhere—not just at the top

When the sun rose on the fields near the city of Jena on October 14, 1806, a mist rolled in and obscured the vision of 200,000 nervous soldiers lined up for battle. Combined with the blinding fog of gun and cannon fire, the armies of Napoleon Bonaparte of France and Frederick William III of Prussia created the opportunity for leadership to prevail over command and control. Command and control leadership is—nothing happens without orders or confirmation from the top.

Though significantly outnumbered, Napoleon routed the Prussians and the Kingdom of King Frederick William III was cut in half and subjugated to the French Empire. The leadership lessons learned that day still guide military leaders around the world and used by leaders in the marketplace with great efficiency and effectiveness.

Both sides observed that the commanders behind the battlefield were unable to see or understand what was happening at the front during the chaos of combat. The people who really knew what was happening were the subordinate officers fighting in the middle of the gun and cannon fire and smoke. The Prussian commanders missed many key opportunities during the fog of battle. Napoleons men, who were faster and more inventive on the battlefield, exploited every opportunity both great and small. The individual genius of front line leaders won the day.

They concluded that the French leaders on the battlefield were reacting much faster to the situation at hand and took the initiative independently without consulting high command. Thus, they quickly exploited any unexpected favorable situation or responded immediately to an unfavorable development without *permission.*

The Prussians knew they had to find a new system of command, one that would enable their field commanders to deliver the same results with a greater degree of flexibility. It would be very different from the rigid and hierarchical command and control philosophy of the time, as much of the leadership is today in many organizations.

The new battle/leadership philosophy was that strict rules and rigid commanders have no place when fighting forces whose field commanders are empowered to make real leadership decisions at the point of live fire. Field commanders must be flexible, innovative, and improvised as long as they stay within the commander's intent.

Once the vision and goals of the senior commander's intent are understood, decisions made in the field no longer have to run up and down the chain of command. Field commanders only maintain the competitive advantage when they are able to exploit positive opportunities that evolve during the heat of battle.

Leadership is not about what your team does when you are around - but how they produce wins when you are not around. If you have to constantly give directives and control the action, you are not leading. If you do not trust the people on your team, then you need to select, teach, train, and coach them better.

If team members do not have all the information they need, know how to perform the "talk" with confidence and understand the expected results, then you as their leader have set them up for failure when they must be at their very best. If you want to "create Leaders everywhere" that maintain a competitive edge, don't ask them to run every decision up and down the chain of command, especially during the "fog of battle."

Success at every level depends on having leaders at every level. Leaders that are able to identify, qualify, and deal quickly and efficiently with difficult and/or unforeseen circumstances. They must be able to take the initiative, while not losing sight of their leader's intent and the goals of the mission.

Top leaders may define success, but it is your leaders on the front lines, with a leadership mindset, that determines it. The leaders in the trenches, not the corner office, win most of the battles. You need both. Let them ignore each other and see how much is accomplished. Everyone in your organization is a leader. They are leading others either closer to the vision or further away by their daily attitude and actions. You can manage actions but never attitudes. That requires resonant leadership!

Utilizing these next seven foundational priorities for creating leaders everywhere will create and maintain a sense of urgency about the future.

Great leaders constantly focus on fulfilling the vision. They inspire their team to do the same. Always focused on future results they resist the urge to allow daily management issues to bog them down and drain their time and energy.

1
Stay Focused on Critical Strategic Issues

Great leaders stay focused on identifying critical strategic issues and creating an action plan to resolve them. They do not focus on today's management. I often say that today's management problems are simply an indication of a previous leadership failure. Teach, train, and empower Managers to solve current problems. Strategic Leaders find and correct leadership failures that created them.

2
Stay Focused on High-Leverage Activities

Great leaders invest their time, resources and energy in activities that produce the greatest return. Spend the lion's share of your leadership influence on developing new leaders—not passionate followers.

Great followers will make today better, but will do little to create a compelling future.

3
Make Tough Decisions an Individual Responsibility at Every Level

Great leaders teach entry- level leaders this priority and skill when they begin their leadership journey. New or inexperienced leaders that do not learn this will fail at higher levels of responsibility. When leaders fail at higher levels, the stakes are greater; the costs more substantial; and the impact on people can be overwhelming.

Making tough decisions is a learned skill needing improvement regardless of your leadership level.

4
They Hold People Accountable - Individually and as a Team

Great leaders create a performance agreement, individually and for the team, that everyone understands. If this agreement does not provide accountability and create energy for the task, it needs to be re-written. It is up to you as the leader to reward and reinforce the behavior and results you desire to see and correct the rest. Lead to achieve a spirit of excellence, and avoid perfectionism at all costs.

If your team does not perform up to expectations, always look first in the mirror, then out the window.

5
Pick the Best Person for the Job

Great leaders are slow to appoint to avoid having to "dis-appoint." The best person may not always be your favorite person. Learn to develop superior judgment when evaluating the potential of an individual to perform.

Have a strong template in evaluating individual leadership skills and performance capability. Leave the position vacant rather than fill it with less than the ideal candidate that may be difficult to remove later.

6
Keep Raising the Standard

Great leaders never stay at the same level - for themselves or their team. They strive for growth and improvement every year. Goals are set for every leader and his team. Promote people on individual and team results - not potential. If you do not ask for more than your team can give, you will never get all they can give. Great leaders have the ability to know when and how to challenge their team so that team can achieve all they are capable of and are ready to handle.

Lesson 27
Seven ways leaders make life easier

When coaching, I often say, "Managers make things complex and Leaders make things simple." When Jesus arrives on the scene, the religious managers had filled the rulebook with at least 365 commandments. Being the greatest leader of all time, he said, *"Let me make things simple; there are just two commandments. And if you keep them, you will fulfill all the others."*

Leaders should always be looking for ways to simplify and make the very complex world in which we live today a little easier for those who look to us for leadership. Here are seven modifications that may help you:

Modify the pace of everyday living

Not everything can or should be #1.

Do not over commit. Say "no" more often.

Relaxation, vacation or sabbatical are not dirty words.

Modify your expectations of yourself and others

Don't let others create your scorecard for success and most of all, your significance.

Unfulfilled expectations still bring life's greatest disappointments. Be led by a spirit of excellence not driven by perfectionism.

Modify your commitments

Projects and events demand both time and energy. Do more with less. Strive to be effective and efficient. Manage your commitments and time will care for itself.

Modify your possessions

Do you own them or just rent them? Cash is still king and debt will sap your life. Get out! You don't have to have the latest or greatest.

Modify your relationships

Hang out with *Balcony People*—avoid *Basement People*. Know the difference between vision makers, vision supporters and vision drainers. Choose wisely. Nurture the makers, develop the supporters and release the drainers. Know where your hospitality saturation point ends and don't go beyond it.

Modify your ministry

Lead your ministry or someday it will be driving you. Managing your ministry is not the same as leading it.

Know your God-given gifts and talents. Find a way to get there, flow there and stay there. Know what you do best. Learn to do it better and how to do more of it. Not every "need" should be a demand on your time.

Modify how you pull it all together

Have a project, event, energy and time management tool. Use it consistently until it becomes a way of life. Start each day with a prioritized "to do" list. Have lifetime, annual, monthly, weekly and daily goals. What are the hurdles and obstacles that prevent you from modifying your life? Write them down and ask God for a strategy to overcome them.

Few leaders make major changes because they are usually not sustainable. But, most of us are capable of making some modifications; slight alterations that if followed consistently with minimal effort, lead to significant changes that are sustainable and make life easier.

Lesson 28
Solving problems or creating the future

Are you solving problems or creating the future? There are two basic kinds of leaders, leaders who solve management problems and leaders who provide strategic leadership for the future. Both are vital for success. It always works best if the leader in charge has strategic planning skills. If not, most likely the organization is bogged down in management challenges, losing forward momentum and stopped pursuing the vision. Soon active inertia sets in and advancing the vision is a discussion item but little else.

Strategic planning is hard work. It requires objectivity and sometimes a painful look in the mirror. Without defining present reality with brutal honesty, you are not ready for the future. Many leadership teams are hesitant to challenge the status quo, change behaviors or execute new procedures. Why?

A "this is the way we have always done it" attitude remains comfortable and nothing changes. The pace of today's changing world and the need to remain relevant demands a strategic planning process.

If you are a senior leader or serve on a core leadership team, strategic planning must be a core value and your primary function. If not, you should move to the management team because chances are you are a problem solver and function better managing the future that others create.

What about your organization, ministry or marketplace effort? Do you focus more on today's problems or tomorrow's opportunities? Do you have a strategy (action plan) that is clear to everyone on your team? Does everyone know the current goals and how they relate to the strategy? Does your structure bring operational value on a daily basis? Do the behaviors of your team members align with your values, goals and strategy?

Why is strategic planning so important? It is, if growth and fulfilling your vision is important. Leaders who say they have a vision but cannot adequately define it always amaze me. They have no defined action plan to get there. Strategic planning brings objectivity and structure to the planning process. It sets the stage and guides the leadership team in a common and focused direction. It provides a road map for success.

Strategic planning directs the investment of resources and provides accountability for results. It's a great way to measure success and return on investment. Good strategic plans, properly executed, include the following:

Bring clarity on your mission, vision and values.
Helps in planning efforts and improve the decision-making process. Help anticipate and productively manage change. Align everyone on priorities and purpose.

Establish performance expectations and identify strengths and weaknesses. Analyze the systems and processes. Create and maintain a culture of constant improvement.

Organizations performing at the highest levels of achievement while maintaining a spirit of excellence do so because they stay engaged in a good strategic planning process. Conversely, a leading cause of organizational failure is the lack of adequate long-range planning tools executed consistently.

Strategic planning, along with many other leadership challenges, always goes better with an outside facilitator or coach. Why do they help things go better?

They bring objectivity and structure to the process.

They bring a sense of urgency to the real issues.

They help clarify and merge competing priorities.

They help identify and eliminate non-productive behaviors.

They challenge assumptions and the statues quo.

They provide options not previously considered.

They help leaders stay focused on solutions - not just problems.

You can create a better today with better management solutions; But, you only create a better tomorrow through a better strategic planning process. As a senior leader, what is your priority?

Lesson 29

The greatest leader Who ever lives

I am often asked about the improper grammar used in my title, "The Greatest Leader Who Ever Lives," should be "...ever lived," past tense. I quickly respond the greatest leader who ever lived is still alive!

Leadership should be everyone's business. Leadership is not about being elected or appointed to a position, nor a place on some organizational flow chart. It's about an attitude of servant hood and a sense of responsibility for making a difference every day wherever God has assigned you.

If you lead in no other way, you're either leading people closer to Christ or further away by the life you live and the example you set in every area of your life. Jesus was the greatest leader and developer of people. He trained twelve human beings who went on to influence a world in such a dramatic fashion that time itself is recorded as B.C. or A.D.

He worked with a staff that was very human - not divine. They were selected from trees, back alleys and along riverbanks. Some were educated and some were illiterate. Some had questionable backgrounds, divisive moments, and times of cowardice. In spite of all this, he trained them and sent them out. They did it for one reason—so they could be with Him again.

Jesus, as a leader, was strong in at least three areas

First—He mastered Himself. He knew who He was. He did not look back from the cross and say, "Wow...I must be the Son of God." In John 10:36, He declared Himself to be the Son of God. He regularly visualized the success of His life and efforts.

You will never master your life or situation until you have mastered yourself. You will never master yourself until you master your tongue. Your words define your future. Jesus was always speaking powerful, loving and confident words about Himself. You will never build people and lead them to victory by tearing yourself down.

Second—Jesus mastered his actions. He said, "I came to do the will of my Father." He took action. Leaders have a bias for action. He had a plan. With the Holy Spirit's guidance, He accomplished all he was sent to do. Too many "leaders" want the help of others and pray fervently for God's help but have no plan. He formed a team. He had the power, authority, and ability to do it alone but instead, chose a team. Someone once said, "Whoever forms a team to carry out the best idea wins."

Third—He mastered His relationships. No matter where you provide leadership, you soon discover how critical relational equity is to success. In Mark 10:21 it says, *"And Jesus beheld the man and looking at him, loved him."* The word "beheld" here means, "to be fully centered, hold or embrace at that moment." How you view people is more important than how you use people.

He gave them a vision larger than themselves and one that would outlast their lifetime. Too many leaders have not figured out how to inspire their followers because the vision is not clear to the entire team, or they have lost the passion to declare it frequently, consistently and with confidence.

He empowered people. Servant leaders constantly ask, "What can I do for you?" Experienced leaders learn that the more you empower those who serve you, the more they want to do for you and faithful longer.

Jesus was the consummate leader because He mastered Himself, His actions and His relationships. Results? He fulfilled His purpose and was able to say, "It is finished." May those you serve you and follow your leadership, do so with the same passion as they followed Him.

Lesson 30
The world is our parish

If the Church, the ecclesia, the called out ones fulfills its mandate *"...make disciples of all nations"* (Matthew 28:19), I believe the following adjustments must take place.

First—our ministry philosophy must change from traditional to biblical. Terms such as clergy, laity, part-time, full-time, called, secular and bi-vocational have contributed to the inability of the Church to see the discipling of entire nations. God never intended for these divisions and distinctions to exist. Especially in light of his desire for the priesthood of all believers described in Exodus 19:6; I Peter 2:5,9 and Revelation 1:6.

His desire has always been a divine partnership for Kingdom expansion made clear in Ephesians. Ephesians 4:1 declares all Christians are called to full-time service as N.T. priests, regardless where that service takes place. Ephesians 4:11 speaks of the "called out ones" from those in Ephesians 4:1. They are given clear instructions. They must equip the 4:1 ministers for the "work of the ministry" in the field of service where God has called them.

Second—our ministry mindset must change from church planting to Kingdom expansion. True church planting is always a by-product of Kingdom expansion in the three entities that control every nation. They are business that creates wealth and drives the economy, governments that pass laws and regulations that maintain order and educational institutions that determine the values and philosophies of every succeeding generation.

Too often, we plant churches and then try to create the demand. Only passionate Ephesians 4:1 ministers answering a divine call and seeing the world as their parish can effectively create that demand. Called marketplace ministers anointed to be there every day do not create in church meetings, conferences, and conventions but in the marketplace the demand for new churches.

Ephesians 4:11 five-fold ministers must teach, train and send Ephesians 4:1 full-time ministers into these ripe harvest fields with a Kingdom mindset, not just a motivation to increase wealth. They need to infiltrate by divine call, elevate by divine favor and eventually dominate these controlling entities via their influence as salt and light. Then the Church has the responsibility to conserve the results of these ministry (not secular) efforts by planting local congregations to do it all over again.

Ministry leadership models must include all five gifts

Third—our ministry leadership model in every local congregation must include all five leadership gifts mentioned in Ephesians 4. Then one anointed leader provides the opportunity for the other four to operate in a spirit of cooperation not competition. Excellence must prevail in the teaching, training and execution of these gifts in an atmosphere of love and faith.

Many claim the title and office, but the impact of their gift leaves a lot to be desired. Leadership is not about authority to command but a passion to serve (Mark 10:45). Great leadership is about influence not command and control. What you cannot accomplish through relationship and influence will never happen through appointed, elected or positional leadership.

Christ's ascension gifts in Ephesians 4 provide oversight to the gifts of the Holy Spirit in Corinthians and Romans. They are given to help every local congregation manage the present and provide leadership for the future. They are as vital to the success of the 21st century Church as they were to the 1st century Church.

Their intended use is just as much for the daily marketplace as for the meeting place on Sunday. They were not for the exclusive use of the five-fold Ephesians 4:11 ministers in the church arena, but just as much for the Ephesians 4:1 ministers doing spiritual warfare in the whitened harvest fields.

Fourth—the leadership team must know how to provide strategic leadership not just management functions. Pastor (the gift) by definition is a manager. The pastoral gift shepherds and cares for the flock.

?one must know how to create a compelling
? the future and that requires a different gift.
All management problems are simply indications of
previous leadership failures, i.e., the BP oil spill,
closed churches and defeated leaders. Only apostolic
leadership gifts can address those issues effectively.

Strategic leadership is all about change

Discipling a nation requires great leaders not
better managers. Great leaders make changes when
they do not have to; good leaders make them when
they have to; and poor leaders are selling tickets after
the train has left the station.

Managers make the rulebook thicker and reigns of authority tighter

If allowed, the managers of every generation
make the rulebook thicker and reigns of authority
tighter. They debate style, form and process. They
discuss the past, debate the present and sometimes
argue about whose interpretation of the future is
correct. All of this does little to change our world in
any significant way. We need good managers to bring
order to the vision strategic leaders create. But, better
management alone will never influence and disciple a
nation. This demands strategic leaders who create
synergy for change around a constantly changing
landscape.

If the world is our parish and if we are commanded to send full-time gospel ministers there to make disciples; then we must understand we cannot manage our way there. The Church must develop strategic leaders who know how to disciple the faithful while developing future strategic leaders in every generation for the marketplace, government and education.

Organizational leaders must seize the moment and inspire those they lead to fulfill these once-in-a-generation opportunities. The world is always one generation away from being evangelized and discipled, if that generation sees the world as their parish and not confine their ministry efforts within the walls of a local church facility.

As Jesus commanded Lazarus loosed from his grave clothes, Ephesians 4:11 ministers must loose their Ephesians 4:1 marketplace ministers from the traditions that have long hindered world evangelism and entire nations from being discipled.

Lesson 31

Three skills all great leaders possess

Great leaders have strong intra-personal and inter-personal leadership skills

These skills are based on character and integrity. They model these skills 24-7, not just when the lights are on.

They have great listening and hearing ability, which are sometimes more important than speaking ability. They know how to create and maintain a constructive dialogue.

They know the difference (and demonstrate) between arrogance and confidence

They appreciate and embrace diversity—cultural, ethnic, economic, educational, and avoid discrimination at all costs. They consistently treat people with respect and dignity regardless of their status in life. They are able to understand, embrace and lead significant change.

Great leaders have strong team building skills

They are able to create a "shared vision." They can build a highly energized and cooperative TEAM around their mission, vision, values and strategy.

They are able to build effective partnerships and alliances within their own ministry and other ministries around the world. They are able to share, without feeling threatened, their leadership influence, impact and results. They are able to recruit, teach, train, deploy and coach quality team players, team leaders and leaders of leaders.

Great leaders have strong strategic planning skills

They possess a "Sons of Issachar" mentality. They understand the times and know what to do. They prepare for an unknown future and plan for as far as they can see and know the difference.

They understand the impact of having a relevant worldview and understand the global landscape. They are able to balance today's ministry challenges while seizing tomorrow's opportunities. They understand, embrace and use emerging technologies. They understand how to use these tools to enhance their ministry's ability to be current and relevant, without compromising their core values. God blesses a supplement but curses a substitute.

They are able to create value for the four stakeholders involved in extending His Kingdom: *Our Heavenly Father*, the One we serve for eternity. *Those we serve every day* with our practical efforts. *Those joining our team* through our discipleship and mentoring efforts. And *those we influence* in the marketplace as salt and light.

Lesson 32

Why ministries & organizations suffer and how to stop the pain

Some call it active inertia, founders' syndrome or just stuck in the past. Whatever you call it, fix it or your organization dies at worst or is ineffective at best. In 1900 the Fortune 100 Companies, best of the best, in 2000 only three remained. What happened to ninety-seven of the top companies just one hundred years later? I believe they suffered from one of the aforementioned diseases.

As with most organizations, by the second or third generation they are over-managed and under-led. How many marketplace companies, churches or Christian organizations do you know one hundred years old or older? It happens in any organized effort involving humans.

Symptoms of the Illness

They are no longer growing and probably losing members. They do not know how to move from entrepreneurial-style leadership to a well-planned and strategically led style.

There is a weak or a strong administrative structure is non-existent. A founder's leadership style of highly reactive, individualistic needs exists and needs to change to more proactive, consensus-oriented style. The organization is experiencing the same recurring problems because of this prevailing style of leadership.

Plans not implemented or seldom succeed most of the time because money and resources scarce. There is an unhealthy turnover in board members and staff. Leadership seems to always to be moving from one crisis to another. Leadership obviously lacks clarity about what is happening when they should know more about what is going on, especially about the future. The funders and supporters base is shrinking and leaderships' is increasingly anxious and defensive.

Traits of Unhealthy Organizations

Founding group is dynamic, driven and decisive. However, these traits are becoming a liability instead of an asset unless they become *mission-minded* instead of remaining entrepreneurial. At the organization's beginning, the leaderships' vision was clear. Their leadership was strong, well connected, and they knew the needs of their members. These strengths have diminished or no longer exist.

Leadership is skeptical about planning, policies and procedures. Reactive and crisis-driven decisions are the norm and not the exception. Believe success solely based on more money and body counts. Board members spend the majority of its time managing the present - not developing strategies for the future.

New leaders feel they are serving the founders more than the mission and vision. Charismatic personalities rather than the mission, vision and values attract new board members and leaders. Leaders motivated more by guilt and pressure than inspiration for the mission and vision.

Leaders cannot let go of, "We've always done it this way and why change." Organization is still personality driven—not process driven.

How to make Sustainable Change that stops the pain and leads to recovery

You develop leaders that display the following traits: They appreciate plans, budgets and guidelines. They make proactive decisions based on mission and budget constraints. They make staff and leadership appointments based on gifting, training, capacities and "coach-ability." They value board members' honest feedback, team spirit and expertise. They sustain credibility among members, vendors and affiliates.

Teach basic principles to present and future leaders: Not all recurring problems are the fault of one individual. Current management problems were first a leadership failure. Be willing to look for and accept help. Do not let your ego and pride keep you in pain. Relieve yourself from having to know everything. Communicate often and honestly based on accurate and adequate information. Be patient with yourself and all others. Take time to reflect and learn from each other.

Board or Leadership Team Actions: Insist on Board member training and orientation. Review roles and responsibilities. Conduct an annual self-evaluation ensuring effectiveness and efficiency. Conduct annual risk management review. Ensure job descriptions and performance agreements are current. Keep reporting simple, regular and effective. Maintain Strategic Planning Process and review annually. Be hope dealers for the leadership and membership. Your words define their future and yours.

Conduct "zero-based" program review. No program is sacred. Abandon if no longer effective in supporting mission. Do not sit on problems or ignore them—solve them.

Summary

What got you where you are will probably not get you where you want to go. Leadership is about change. Let the past go and find out what it going takes to move forward. Envision where you want to be in five years and devise a plan to get there.

Remember, "Accurate, adequate and shared information coupled with open and honest communication is the only way to make informed decisions." It takes courage, determination and a spirit of cooperation to honestly define present reality and devise a strategy for recovery and forward progress.

Without outside wisdom and coaching, recovery is difficult for any organization, regardless of size, resources, leadership expertise or longevity.

Lesson 33

Your City—God's kind of town—A declaration of destiny

We believe our city is God's kind of town. He died for our city on the cross. When he took his last breath, he thought of our city. When he emerged victorious from the tomb he did so for our city.

He had our city on his mind when he sent His disciples to the far reaches of the world. He is coming for the citizens of our city who await His return; who have pledged allegiance beyond the limits of our city to His Eternal City and everlasting Kingdom.

In the meantime, we are called to a great task. We reach our city one soul at a time. It's not an easy assignment, but doable with His grace and power. Our city is a battleground, not a playground. It's a city the enemy has staked out as his territory.

We now declare God's intent, and our destiny, for the city we love and are called to serve. We will not allow the enemies of our God and King to have one more inch of our city. We are here to declare victory and open her up as an outpost of God's eternal Kingdom.

Our church has been called to open up deaf ears to the Good News of the Gospel. We have been summoned to open up prison doors for spiritual captives. We have been ordered by our King to open our arms to people of all races. We have been commanded to open our hearts to the poor, the needy and the suffering.

We are in this city to open up the Word of God to the spiritually ignorant. We are here to open up the hearts of all Christians for evangelism and encouragement. We have been commissioned to build the altar of God in the center of our government, educational institutions and the marketplace.

We believe this is God's intent and our destiny, but we cannot do it alone or in our own strength. We are empowered by the Holy Spirit. Thus we declare our intent to seek God until He visits our church and our city again with a fresh Pentecostal outpouring that adds to his church daily.

We open our ears and hearts to hear the voice of God and His message for our generation. We open our dusty prayer closets to seek His face as never before. We open our schedules to Divine appointments He brings us every day.

We open our wallets and purses and sow seeds that bring an eternal harvest. We pray for a fresh wind of the Holy Spirit to blow through our lives, our church and our city. Blow away anything that hinders the full expression of God's demonstrated love for our city. Heavenly Father, our city is your kind of town.

In the mighty name of your Son, we declare war against Satan and sin. We are not here to engage in a skirmish or retreat after a single battle – but to do war until you come back.

Fill us with your Spirit. Empower us by Your Word. Dress us with your divine armor. We are poised within our city to strike upon your command. Make bare your mighty arm on our behalf and we shall present our city to you as a jewel for your everlasting crown on that day - the Great Day of the Lord. Amen!

Lesson 34

Your gift makes room for you

All effective ministry service, church or marketplace, is based on exercising your gifts to the *"glory of God."*

"Whether you drink, eat, do – do for glory of God." —I Corinthians 10:31

"Whatever you do, word or deed, do it in the name of the Lord Jesus, giving thanks to God the Father through Him." —Colossians 3:17

"If you speak, do it as one speaking the very words of God—so that in all things God is praised through Jesus Christ – to Him be the glory and power forever." —I Peter 4:11

The Fruit of the Spirit validates your spiritual gifts, prepares recipients and maximizes effectiveness because gifts are useless without fruit.

Galatians 5:22: *"But the fruit the Spirit is Love..."* Love is manifested eight ways; joy, peace, longsuffering, kindness, goodness, faithfulness, gentleness and self-control.

Your Walk with God Prepares You and Motivates You to Use Your Gift

"Enoch walked with God till he was not."

Walking is deliberate.
Walking is regulated.
Walking requires trust.
Walking is learned.
Walking is progressive.

Key: Colossians 2:6: "As you received Christ, so walk in Him." You walk with God before you walk with brothers. You walk with brothers before you walk among heathen.

Your Spiritual Gifts Enable You for Ministry

Because you God gifted you does not mean you are ready to operate in that gift. You must exercise and develop your gift under the watchful eye of a seasoned mentor before demonstrating it to others. Keep in mind the following: Gifts do not cause fruit to grow. God gives the gifts—you have to grow your own fruit.

It is *"Not by might or power—but by Spirit says the Lord."* Mature Christians, yield to God thus, they are more confident. People with same gifts can express them differently.

Your Heart Passions Keep Your Gift Focused

How your heart is drawn—should determine your focus.

What energizes you?
What concerns you?
What do you think is important?
What pulls your heartstrings?

Passions center around 3 categories:

1. People Groups: age, gender, social status, nationality, lifestyle, marital status.
2. Ministry Areas: worship, teaching, fellowship, outreach.
3. Issues and Causes: social, church life, family life.

Key: I Thessalonians 2:8: *"We loved you so much that we were delighted to share with you not only the Gospel of God, but our lives as well – because you had become so dear to us."*

Your Gift Expressed Through Personality

Understand and embrace WHO you are and WHO you are not. Understand how you relate to yourself and how you relate to others—through your personality temperament. What makes you tick and what ticks you off and how you handle pressure and conflict.

Explains why some things in life come easier to others.

How you build relational equity.

Leadership Style.

Servant Attitude.

Communicate/Speaking.

Your Life Experience Develops Your Ministry Gift(s)

a. *Romans 8:28: "And we know that all things work together for God's good— for those who love Him and called according to His purpose."*

b. God uses your experiences to develop you for He created you.

c. "In everything give thanks . . . "

d. Romans 8:18-39

1. (Vs. 18-25)—Life is not always easy but it's never without hope.

2. (Vs. 26-27)—We are not alone.

3. (V. 28)—Life experiences are always for our greater good.

4. (Vs. 29-30)—God's ultimate goal, conforming us to His image.

5. (Vs. 31-34)—God will protect, guide and build you up. The Holy Spirit and Christ are praying for you.
6. (Vs. 35-39)—Regardless of what comes, we are more than conquerors.

Your Assignment Utilizes Your Gift(s)

a. Do what you were created, gifted, called and anointed to do by God and learn to say *no* if not.
b. Need does not always determine call.
c. Hardest ministry you will ever do is the one you were not called to do.

God's Favor Endorses and Opens Doors for Your Ministry Gifts

Proverbs 18:16—"A man's gifts makes room for him, and brings him before great men."

Matthew 3:17—"This is my beloved Son—well pleased."

Positions, titles and offices may open some doors—but only God opens the right doors.

Lesson 35
Seven marks of a great finisher

THEY FUNCTION AS A STRATEGIC LEADER AND UTILIZE TEAMWORK.

I see so many senior leaders who don't understand their role as a strategic leader. They are bogged down in day-to-day management. Whatever shows up on their radar screen is where they focus. If you have strategic (future) leadership responsibilities, your primary function is communicating (not managing or controlling) the mission, vision and values. If you don't, who will? Your secondary role is knowing your team members, individually and as a team. Team work becomes the primary way of pursuing the vision and reaching goals.

They define present reality with brutal honesty

Ministries are full of people who do not want to deal with present reality much less with brutal honesty. The reasons are many. It makes people uncomfortable; want to hide or downplay mistakes; avoid confrontation, or simply live in denial are just a few.

As a leader, if you refuse to define present reality with brutal honesty, you are not ready to move to the future, whether it is this afternoon, next week, next month or next year. You cannot paint a picture for what you want (called vision) if today's reality is vague in your mind and the team's.

They establish clear and compelling goals

I have coached many leaders who, when we start, cannot tell what they are going to do next (as it relates to their vision) and why. Most leaders wake up every day with 50 gorillas facing them. They cannot deal with all of them but without clear and compelling goals, most burn out trying.

If you have more than two to three new goals for the year, you have too many. If everything is a priority, nothing becomes the priority. You will be bogged down in details and another year will pass without progress.

Every day, week, and month should have goals that support your annual goals. If they are not compelling to you, you can be sure they will not be for your team.

They make follow-through a way of life

Setting clear and compelling goals matters little if no one takes them seriously. Everyone may agree that it's a great goal/idea but it will not happen unless someone is held responsible for the results.

If there are no consequences for lack of following through and getting the desired results, then do not expect much to change. However, before you start holding people accountable, make sure they have been taught so they understand; trained so they can perform competently; given adequate resources; and kept inspired by you, their leader. Only then do you have the right to hold them accountable for the agreed upon results.

They grow well-rounded team members

Being a positional, appointed or elected leader and a leader who builds a great team following a compelling vision are not the same. Developing emotionally mature team members has never been a greater challenge for leaders. The pace and pressures of life for everyone has intensified.

You need to spend at least 40% of your available time developing the top 15-20% of your leaders. *"And Jesus increased in wisdom, stature and favor with God and man."* (Luke 2:52) That is still a great model to follow.

If you want to develop this type of team member, you must find time apart from the task. Relationships built only around the task usually lead to burnout or bailout. If they know, you trust them and believe in them for who they are, not just, for what they can do, most will always give you 100% regardless of the effort or the demands you place on them.

They understand rewards and sanctions and get them right

Only pass these out after you have taught them to understand; trained them to perform competently; and only then can you coach them to excellence. Telling someone to do something is not the same as teaching, training and coaching. Many times, you pass out rewards and sanctions prematurely with little if any, long-term results. Make your standards and expectations for both clear, firm and fair.

They don't kid themselves

Someone once said, "To thine own self be true." Without emotional maturity, you will never be totally honest with yourself or others. If you or those on your team do not follow through with the plan, then do something about it. One of the worst things you can do is kid yourself into believing you can be a great leader without follow-through.

Being a good leader is not the same as giving leadership where following through is never an option. Great leaders come to grips with their own weaknesses. They deal with them honestly and move on. However, lack of follow-through should never qualify as an acceptable weakness. Do not tolerate it for yourself or anyone on your team. If you do, do not expect your goals to be met and do not be disappointed when they are not.

The Apostle Paul said, *"I have finished my course."* You may not win every race and see every goal met but at least you should be able to say, "I finished and we finished!"

"JUST DO IT!"

Lesson 36
How great leaders make good decisions

Good judgment and making good decisions is the fundamental essence of leadership, especially when the stakes are high, information is limited and the best decision is far from obvious.

The ability to make good judgment calls (the thought and analysis process), followed by choosing the best decision (putting your judgment into action) is not an inborn trait, but skill developed, fine-tuned and nurtured by great leaders at all levels.

Judgment resides at the core of leadership. Judgment is informed decision making taking place in three areas: people, strategy, and during crisis or challenge. Within each area, leadership judgment follows a three-phase process: preparation, decision, and execution.

Leaders are remembered for three things, the problems they solve, the problems they create, and their best and worst judgment calls. In the face of ambiguity, uncertainty, and conflicting demands, the quality of a leader's judgment determines not only present reality, but also the future success or failure.

It is important to recognize the critical moment before a judgment call (when swift and decisive action is essential) and how to execute the decision.

What you will learn in this study: A useful framework for making better decisions and helping shape your team to do the same. Addressing the toughest questions leaders face when making their most important judgments.

Improving your decision-making abilities; why are some leaders better equipped to deal with crisis?

Framework For Leadership Judgment

Getting the important decisions right:

1. Cumulative effect of leader's judgment calls determines the effectiveness of   your leadership at best and failure at worst.

2. You add value by how well you make good decisions under time pressure, in a crisis or challenge or when facing uncertainty and conflicting demands.

3. What makes or breaks a leader are not how *many* judgments they make or even what *percentage* they get right, but how many of the *important* ones they get right.

5. Great leaders are better at the whole process that runs from seeing the need for a judgment call to framing the issue to figuring out what is critical to mobilizing and energizing the troops.

Three Phases in the Judgment-Making Process

Time, this includes what happens before the leader makes the decision. What the leader does as he makes the decision that helps it turn out to be the right one. What the leader must oversee to make sure the call produces the desired results.

Areas, there are three critical areas in which the majority of the most important decisions are made people, strategy (action plan) and times of crisis or challenge.

Resources, decisions are not (or should not) be made in isolation but in relationship to the *real world*. A leader's network (relationships) is the source of information needed to make a successful decision. Leaders must learn to interact successfully with four types of knowledge:

1. Self-Knowledge
2. Social Network Knowledge
3. Organizational Knowledge
4. Contextual Knowledge

Three judgment areas

People Judgment Decisions: Without good people decisions, there is no way leaders can set a clear and healthy direction for the ministry or effectively deal with crisis or challenge.

Strategy Judgment Decisions: Great leaders are always leading the organization to a successful future. When the current path (strategic direction) is not leading toward health and success, it is their responsibility and primary duty to do so. How well a leader makes strategic judgments calls is a function of both: Their ability to look over the horizon, frame the critical issues and ask the right questions.

The resources and people they choose to interact with and engage in the process.

Crisis or challenge judgment decisions: These calls require that a leader have clear values, compelling mission and vision statements, and clarity about the ultimate goal. Crisis or challenges when good judgments and decisions are not made, can lead to the downfall of the best organizations and ministries.

The process of making a good decision

In all three areas: people, strategy, and crisis or challenge good judgment calls always involve a process that starts with recognizing the need for a call and continues through to successful execution of the decision. This process involves three phases:

The Preparation Phase

This phase includes sensing and identifying the need for a judgment call; framing the issues needed to make the call; and mobilizing and aligning the right people and resources.

The Call Phase

There is a "moment of truth" based on the leader's view of the time line for the judgment call; sufficiency of input and analysis; involvement of others, the leader decides to make the call.

The Execution Phase

Making it Happen: Execution is where most leaders and organizations fail—primarily because they failed in the prior two phases. Once you make a clear call then mobilize and align resources, people, information and technology to support it. If not, the decisions made will simply fail. Good judgment always produces good (not always perfect) results.

Resources and Relationships

The quality of a leader's decision-making ability depends a lot on their ability to marshal resources and develop a network of relationships. Most of the time, these will overlap. A great leader develops and uses four types of knowledge to make good judgments.

1. Self-Knowledge: Great leaders understand, accept, and try to improve their E.Q. They are able to listen as well as see. They are able to adjust and reframe their thinking and give up old models, if necessary.

2. First there is the area of relationship Network Knowledge: Leadership is a team sport, not individual stars. There must be alignment of team and key stakeholders if you are going to create and increase the capacity to make good judgments and decisions. Leaders must: Intentionally work to encourage teamwork. Draw on the best resources of each team member. Help team members make better judgments in their own areas of responsibility.

3. Then there is Organizational Knowledge: Good leaders work hard to enhance the team, organizational and stakeholder capacity at all levels to make good judgments.

4. And then Stakeholder Knowledge: Good leaders engage partners, suppliers, related boards and committees in generating knowledge to make better judgments.

How Great Leaders Make Good Decisions

How depends a lot on who the leader is. Great leaders who consistently make the best judgment calls do the following:

Have a clear mental framework to guide their thinking. Have stories running in their heads about how the ministry works, and an *end in view* picture of how they want to turn out.

They possess the all-important qualities of character, integrity, and courage.

They have the internal discipline to make the right call and follow it through.

Great Leaders are Teachers

They lead their ministry through teaching and they develop other teaching leaders. They use their valuable knowledge and experience to convey ideas, proposals, and ultimate vision. They use their values to energize others to help them make clear, decisive and good decisions.

Transformational leaders know how to weave this knowledge, experience, and values into their story line until it becomes a reality.

Examples: Dr. Martin Luther King and the Apostle Paul.

Great Leaders' Storylines Address Three Issues

Where are we now?

Why are we going now? Adds motivation for change or movement; lights the way and defines the goal.

How are we going to get there? The storyline is never complete, but always evolving and being modified by future judgments. The storyline is what keeps the judgments from being isolated and disconnected acts that may or may not move the organization forward.

Great Decision Makers' Eternal Qualities

Character: This means having values and a moral compass that set clear standards for what you will or will not do. Character is all about knowing right from wrong and setting these parameters long before facing tough judgment calls. It is about knowing what your goals are and sticking with them.

Integrity: This word describes not only a person who has values and principles that are above reproach, but are integrated and form the whole of a leader's character and personality and how they provide leadership.

Courage: Judgment is about more than decision-making. It is about not only finding the right solution to the right problem, but about producing results. This is where courage comes in.

Having courage to act on your standards is critical to making good judgments for the long haul. If you do not act on your *standards*, there is some question as to whether they really are your standards.

It is the courage to take the "high road," which most of the time is the "hard road" littered with obstacles, simply because you *should*.

Trust: This is the emotional glue holding teams together. Lack of character, integrity, and courage, is the quickest way to lose trust or never get it in the first place. Leaders who have these internal qualities have some distinct advantages:

They are easier to trust and follow.

They honor commitments and promises.

Their "walk" matches their "talk."

They are always engaged with present reality in their ministry and informed about the world in which their stakeholders live and work.

They remain open to "reflective feedback."

They willingly admit errors and learn from their mistakes.

They speak with passion because they believe in what they are saying.

They feel at ease in the leadership position and energized by being there.

They tend to be more open to opportunity and risk.

People Judgment Calls

People calls are complex: To make good people judgments, a leader has to do the following:

Recognize your present reality and know how it relates to the future. Frame the issues until everyone understands and connects personally. Mobilize and align the team and resources including the information and wisdom needed to make good decisions and judgment calls.

People judgments are complex because judgment about whether someone will be a good leader is a judgment call about how well the person will do making his or her own judgment calls. Will they be able to build a good team?

Develop effective strategy (plans for the future)

Deal with the inevitable crisis and overwhelming challenge.

People judgments always involve emotions: Leaders are human. They have feelings, emotions, and flawed personalities.

They become attached to people or find them hard to understand and sometimes hard to accept. This lack of objectivity makes it difficult to make good people calls.

People judgments always come first: Without a team of trusted leaders, it will be impossible to make good strategy judgments.

People politics will always undermine what is best for the ministry, especially during times of crisis and great challenge.

People Judgment Calls During Transition

Who leads an organization or ministry is the single most important people judgment.

A long-term commitment needs made for developing a pool of leaders at all levels_ensuring a flow of leaders for the future. Future senior leaders are discovered, developed and deployed in opportunities with lesser responsibilities and more opportunity for failure.

Empty leadership pools are caused by: Lack of disciplined planning process for leadership development and neglect by present Senior *Leadership Teams* to provide for the future of the ministry.

Poor understanding of present reality, future leadership requirements, ego issues, ineffective leaders not wanting to let go, and other issues contributing to a lack of or poor leadership transitions.

Six Keys For Making Good People judgments

Anticipate the need for key people changes.

Clarify the leadership requirements and expectations, looking into the future, not the rearview mirror. Mobilize and align your relationship network to support the right call.

Make the process transparent and judged fairly

You must pull the trigger to make it happen. You also must provide continuous support and adequate follow-up to help the new leader succeed.

Strategy Judgments

Strategy development is not an event but an ongoing process for true leaders. Keeping the vision fresh and alive by telling your story is critical.

Vision casting means continuously revising and making clear what is in your heart and mind while good decisions are made along a changing pathway.

The ability to be flexible and willing to write and rewrite your storyline by making sound judgments is how successful leaders make successful change and transformation.

Good strategic judgment is caused by: leader's capacity and capability to frame the ministry's opportunities and challenges. The ministry's potential are always resources and people. Leader's ability to mobilize aligns key leaders and influencers to help make smart judgments followed by active decisions.

Strategy judgment require:

1. A Process
2. Preparation
3. A Call (Decision)
4. An execution

NOTE: Strategy judgments alter where the organization is heading. They require leaders to have clear teaching values, a compelling storyline (vision), and courage to make the calls and the perseverance to execute and follow through, along with the ability to conceptualize the future.

Crisis And Challenge judgments

A. Good judgments made during times of crisis and challenge follow the same process as judgments made during times of less stress. There is a preparation phase, a call phase and an execution phase. However, the preparation phase is before the crisis or challenge.

B. Great leaders prepare for the crisis before it occurs. Examples: Katrina and 9-11.

C. Leaders generally either make bad judgments because they lack a teaching style of leadership; a good storyline; or have made poor people judgments.

D. To handle crises and challenges effectively, leaders must have an aligned team. Otherwise, a crisis will splinter the team just when you need smart and coherent action the most.

Bad people or strategy judgments can cause a crisis. But once it happens, teamwork and focus make all the difference between survival and disaster.

Crisis/Challenge Requires Leadership Capabilities

Why are some leaders better equipped to deal with crisis and challenge than others do?

A. They anticipate crises. They clearly understand they come to all leaders and they prepare themselves and their team to respond effectively and efficiently—not react.
B. These leaders understand that to survive and perhaps come out ahead in times of crisis, you must have three things:

1. An aligned and trusted team.
2. A clear teaching set of values and storyline (vision) for the ministry's future success.
3. A firm commitment to developing other leaders throughout the crisis or challenge.

Great Leaders Create And Maintain A Learning Environment

First imperative of great leaders who make good judgments is a commitment to be a learner, keep developing one's knowledge and wisdom. "Readers are leaders." They invest heavily in leadership development in their other team members.

Self-Knowledge Creation: means great leaders are on a transformational journey beginning with themselves and this passion carries over to their team. To do this, leaders need the paradoxical combination of self-confidence and humility to learn.

It has to be a priority and passion of leaders who aspire to be good leaders and provide great leadership. It takes commitment to self-learning, significant time, and a relentless willingness to "look in the mirror" not just out the window.

A burning desire to be the best God intended you to be

Relationship Network Knowledge Creation: Every leader relies on a team of trusted advisors. You spend most of your time with these people. When difficult judgments arise, they convene their team to debate, deliberate, and decide.

Building a relational network that keeps developing their knowledge creation capacity is central to the success of a leader.

Organization Knowledge Creation: Helping leaders at all, levels strengthen their ability to make good judgments that are best for the overall ministry—not just their individual or departmental concerns.

All leadership development from new stakeholders through senior leaders needs is geared toward gaining the knowledge and experience to make better decisions and judgments.

Contextual Knowledge Creation: Increasing your ability to work with stakeholders, governing groups, guests and the communities in which your ministry operates.

Leaders need to develop clear and user-friendly processes and systems for developing knowledge about the context of your ministry and those affected by it.

Conclusion

The process of judgment and decision-making begins with the leader recognizing the need for a judgment and continuing through successful execution.

Leaders are said to have *"good judgment"* when they repeatedly make judgment calls that turn out well. In addition, these calls often turn out well because they have mastered a complex process that unfolds in several dimensions: time, domains and relationships.

Lesson 37
Four tools that determine success

There are four statements (tools) great leaders to define, guide, and determine success, regardless of the effort. They are Mission, Vision, Values and Strategy statements. The following types of leader should lead all organizations:

Mission-ary: one sent on an assignment with apostolic gifting.

Vision-ary: one who sees potential, possibility and options for success.

Mission: defines your assignment – *Provides Direction.*

Vision: reveals what the "final frame" looks like—*Provides Focus.*

Values: are uncompromising and guiding principles feeding your vision—*Provides Nurture.*

Strategy: goal oriented action plan supporting your mission and vision—*Provides Action.*

Your Mission Statement

Our organization exists to do *what*?
For *Whom*?
Where?
For *What Purpose*)?

The verbs in a Mission Statement should be inactive.

Your Vision Statement

Our organization will accomplish our Mission by doing the following. List at least three actions.

1. _____

2. _____

3. _____

The verbs in a Vision Statement are active. They are daily or regular actions that bring you closer to the vision.

Your Values Statement

Values are the soil in which the *seeds of your vision* either flourish and grow or flounder and die. Everything you do should have value, but not everything can be a core value. Pick 5-7 that give you the greatest return on accomplishing your mission and fulfilling your vision.

Your Strategy—Action Statement

1. List your current goals.

2. What process did you use to set them?

3. How realistic are they—ambitious or conservative?

4. How do they compare to last year?

5. What actions (activities) are you implementing to reach your goals? Who is going to do what by when? *WHO*: Do they have the skills, passion, and availability?

- *WHAT*: Do the actions/activities have measurable outcomes?

How will they be measured (accountability) by whom? Do they support the goals?

- *WHEN*: Is there a *Critical Path* to completion? Are there established benchmarks along the way? Is there a *Drop Dead* date for completion?

Summary: If you do not have these statements (tools) and use them consistently, please answer the following statements: What guides your decision-making process?

What creates your focus—expends resources including money, people, time and energy?

How do you create and define "wins" or future success?

How do you measure the efforts of your team?

How do you energize your team (make them tick)?

How do you know when you de-energize your team (tick them off)?

How do you know when your goals are met?

Lesson 38

Kill the organization before the organization kills the ministry

THESIS: If you spend more than one-third of your time, energy, and resources on organizational issues and concerns, you have an organization that exists to support an organization—not an organization that exists to support a ministry.

"Every act of creation is first of all an act of destruction" Picasso

INTRODUCTION: Think about it; at your *leadership* meetings do your team members discuss ministry goals, future opportunities, vision, etc., or do them spend most of their time and energy on *management* issues. Leadership teams in any organization exist to apply all available resources (facilities, finances, personnel) toward Spirit-revealed goals with Spirit-empowered energies.

Organizational managers exist to manage and administer those resources through the *housekeeping* structure, systems, employees and volunteers, based on the accepted values and standards.

Constant awareness of this simple distinction between *managing* and *leading*, so often forgotten, ignored, or simply by-passed because of pressing management concerns, is the key to keeping strategic *leadership teams* focused on "keeping the main thing the main thing."

When all *stakeholders* keep this in mind, they stay focused on why they are keeping house, and not overly focused on how they are keeping house.

Five things to know when you have strategic leadership responsibility.

I. Organize For the Future

The best place to look for the reason(s) for organizational change is in the future ministry and the worst place to look is in the current organizational activities.

The *present organization* is generally a poor predictor of the kind that needed for the future. You should always organize for the *yet-to-be ministry*. Get the best possible fix on what the ministry should look like in five years and design what kind of organization it will take to support that ministry. Prepare for the future organization and a plan of action to get there.

The *present organization* is probably a good indicator of what will prevent you from developing the kind of organization you will need for future ministry goals and needs. Like all creatures, the present organizational structure has a stake in staying the same.

Organizations (people) by nature want to remain at their present level of comfort. The older it becomes—the less it wants to adjust or change.

Rather than investing a lot of time and energy in trying correcting what we believe is wrong and negative in our current *"way of doing things,"* focus on understanding what your *future ministry* should look like. Let your organizational changes support those needs.

II. Create New Ministry Models—Not New Organizational Models

It is better to solve organizational problems by creating new ministries than by focusing solely on the organizational structure. Figure out what the new ministry/service is and organize to fit that—not the other way around.

Strip away refinements and ornaments that *just happen* with any mature organization.

Four *life cycles* of any ministry/organization

Gestation: Venture Capitalists
Growth: Entrepreneurs
Maturity: Offspring/New idea people
Aging: Takeover types—or die.

New organizations or ministries require investment for future payoffs.

Stars: Fast-growing/rapid change types
Cows: Milked through maturity
Dogs: Aging—value added questionable.

Mature organizations do not hatch many, if any, *entrepreneurs-types*. Usually, they resist them strongly because they do not want to do anything about change except to say they need to change.

When the growth curve has flattened over an extended period ... the ability to *give life* has probably passed. At that point, you become content with only sustaining life.

III. Managing Organizational Life-Cycles

Shed the belief that ministries and organizations are immortal in their original form and methods. Mission and Values seldom change but how you deliver your service changes or you find yourself still selling buggy whips in an aerospace world.

Ask the tough questions and informal questions about how management and organizational strategies must change given the acceptance of "A".

Given the answers to "B" the reality of where you are in relation to that reality, ask the question "*What are we doing now to birth the next generation's organizational structure?*"

Ministries at the beginning of their life cycle tend to be under-organized, while those at the mature end of their curve tend to be over-organized. The former seldom use consultants while the latter use them regularly.

Theoretically, there is a place of perfect balance but ideally; you should always be ahead of the organization, not vice-versa. Leadership of older organizations should allow internal information turbo-chargers and entrepreneurs to fight spreading bureaucracy that always sap strength and vitality.

Senior Leaders and Managers should encourage the new generation of leaders at the front of the next life cycle create their own forms of organizational structure and methods of delivering the ministry or services. If they do not change, the mission and values let them fly away from the nest, even if in a new direction.

If top leaders cannot invigorate the ministry functions and new opportunities, stop wasting resources and time attempting to invigorate the present organization.

The most effective organizations are those matched to the same point in their life cycle as the ministry they serve.

Do you have the right bus?

Do you have the right people on the bus?

Do you have the right people, on the right bus, in the right seat?

These questions are sometimes as important, if not more so, than who is driving the bus!

IV. Grow and Reproduce or Die

Death may take decades but it surely comes unless a ministry evolves to a new form, develops a new logic capable of organizing and administering the growth cycles at an increasing level of complexity.

While growth is the key to life within a single life cycle—reproduction is the key to life across a succession of life cycles.

Living things only grow if they continue to differentiate themselves internally ... but all growth has limitations. Growth ends when you reach those limits, maturity begins and eventually aging sets in and decline follows. To continue growing you must figure out a new logic, patterns or design relevant to its mission and target audience.

You must re-invent—not re-gift yourself!

Most mature ministries resist change, or at best, concentrate their efforts on refining rather than re-defining their function, purpose, etc.

KEY: *Because of information technology and market place availability, all ministries are electronically linked, upstream to other organizations, downstream to its members, and laterally in both strategic and global alliances.*

Despite emerging technology, many ministries refuse to develop models to manage this inter-organizational reality. Older, not necessarily mature, ministries fight it. All efforts to change and manage change, if it happens at all, are internal, what were about, it's usually all about us! You let the next generation worry about the future while you eat up the resources and any momentum built up.

You must diligently look for opportunities to develop the distribution and delivery aspects of who we are, what we can provide up and down the links.

V. A New Model For The 21ST Century

You must look for ways to move passive members into entrepreneurial partners. As leaders, you have the responsibility to provide easy and legitimate entry points where all stakeholders can make significant contributions.

When the focus of a ministry is internal, the only way to gain access and have influence is by getting on the governing boards. In most second and third generation ministries that is very difficult.

When the focus is on the front-line ministry, the members in the field, the way to gain influence is through providing top-notch services. Organizations need to be seamless and transparent. Like computers, successful organizations must learn to be easy to use, friendly, seamless and transparent.

1.   Aware of your limitations and realities you face every day you adjust your model for providing services to your members.

2. Move your organization to be flat, flexible, and built around teams—not solo personalities.

3. You spend less time re-modeling and just build a new model.

4. In the meantime, when old models are not working and new models are yet to evolve. What are you to do?

CONCLUSION: Focus on the organizational services and less on organizational structure. Old models will give way to new models in the inevitable cycle of destruction and creation—if leadership will provide the opportunities.

You must stop propping up the old models. Let them go gently into the night ... in spite of those voices that always go kicking and screaming into the future. You can't ride on tracks you haven't laid down!

"Toto, I have a feeling we're not in Kansas anymore." —Dorothy, in "The Wizard of Oz"

Lesson 39
Fear of failure creates hesitant leaders

The fear of failure is the number one cause for not setting goals. It's also the number one reason preventing many leaders from winning where it matters most. You always learn more from failure than success. Success builds confidence—if you learn from it. Failure builds your faith—if you learn from it. In the end, it's not about winning and losing but about learning. The gap between winning and losing is where real learning takes place. However, you must utilize what you have learned not just discuss what did or didn't take place.

Average leaders are usually just as smart and talented as great leaders, but great leaders simply exercise more confidence and courage. Courage and confidence go together if you want to win on a frequent basis.

Great leaders know how to instill the same confidence and courage they have in their team. They allow no superstars, regardless of how gifted or talented, because they know Superstars never win championships. Winning requires a team. You win or lose as a team, seldom as individuals.

There must be a bond of trust keeping a team together and focused on the same vision and common purpose. Great leaders listen, learn and then lead. Inexperienced or arrogant leaders reverse the process and then complain about the lack of cooperation or commitment. Listening well requires walking in a spirit of humility. Too many leaders are talking or telling, when they should be listening and learning. You can never lead your team to where they need to be until you first understand where they are from their perspective, not yours.

How do they feel when you are with them? Do they feel affirmed and empowered or threatened and intimidated? Great leadership is about grace, the ability to rise above and anchored in true humility by always focusing first on others.

Great leadership is always about others—"Look what the team accomplished."

Good leadership is about us—"Look what we did."

Poor leadership is about me—"Look what the team helped me do."

Great teams are people equally committed to one common purpose and who understand what is critical for success. Leaders of great teams are passionate about using the team's effort in bringing individual fulfillment. There are no losers on a winning team, just as there are no superstars, including the leader.

Leadership is not blindly stumbling into tomorrow but combining confidence in your team's past victories with the courage in going for a new win. Do not allow past failures or the possibility of failure lurking in the unknown, cause you to hesitate and miss a great opportunity. Learn from your mistakes and use them to help define future success. Above all, keep moving forward.

Lesson 40
Seven steps for making new things happen

Set Measurable Goals

Never underestimate the high price you pay for pursuing undefined goals. Only 3% of the people in the world set definable goals with an action plan to reach them. The other 97% work for those who do.

Every team member needs to understand exactly what's expected of him or her personally and for the team he or she plays on. There must be a clear definition of the expected results and a pro-active strategy for achieving them. Everyone must know the "score" at all times. Otherwise, how will you know if you win?

Engage a Seasoned Coach and Mentor

Experienced coaches or mentors will help you with the following things:

They keep everyone focused on the goals without present efforts suffering.

They provide timely and constructive feedback.

They create an environment of trust and accountability. They encourage and guide leaders who encounter resisters (people) and obstacles (internal and external challenges).

They use their experience and knowledge of the marketplace, church world, communication, and people, to develop and sustain good working relationships.

They understand that effectiveness is gained through influence and relational equity - not command and control-style leadership or non-relational consulting. They help develop focused and productive action plans. They are prepared to offer opinions but not impose them.

Excellence in Communication

One of my favorite mantras is, "Accurate, adequate and shared information, coupled with open and honest communication, is the only way to make informed decisions." Learn how to communicate - not just talk.

Great leaders understand the difference between communication and information. You can offer too much information, but you can never "over-communicate." Every opinion counts, every voice heard, and clarity is paramount - every time and all the time. What matters is defined, repeated, and pursued passionately. If you don't define what matters, you won't do what matters.

Create and Maintain a Positive Work Environment

People want to join a team with a positive mindset, a culture of trust and accountability, high morale, and a joy to work with. Big and small wins are regularly recognized, celebrated, and awarded-for individuals and for teams.

Individual and Team Accountability

Individuals and teams are accountable for results, not just activity. Leaders model the desired level of accountability by following through on promises.

Everyone has Opportunity to Grow and Improve

Great leaders always resource their team with teaching, training, coaching, finances, equipment and significant learning opportunities. They clear the path forward, keep the goals focused, and ensure everyone wins. They maximize synergy all the time. No superstars or loners allowed.

Build Trust: the Glue of Every Team and the Lubricant of Every Win

There is a culture of trust—not just acts of trust. You build trust by the following:

Shared accountability.
Shared commitments.

Open and honest communication based on accurate information.

No secrets and no surprises.

DWYSYWD: *"Do what you say you will do."*

Great leaders retain the best of the past, combine it with the relevant opportunities of today, and create a better future by leading positive change. When things no longer change under your leadership, you are not leading - you are managing. If that's you - find a leader to follow. There is always a need for good managing leaders. Without them, strategic leaders could create the future.

"Circumstances are the rulers of the weak; but they are the instruments of the wise." —Samuel Glover

Lesson 41
Seven keys for leading sustainable change

Most leaders desire change but only a few are willing to learn what it takes and how to implement productive and sustainable change. If you are tired of the status quo and want things to change for your organization here are seven keys that will help:

Create a Sense of Urgency

Strategic leaders create the future and managing leaders guide the daily affairs. Leaders determine direction and focus, while managers watch the performance and determine the numbers. Together, they must create a sense of urgency strong enough to overcome the status quo and change present reality.

Create a Vision for Change

Good ideas and talking points should never substitute for setting goals.

Until you set measurable goals, change is never significant or sustainable.

Sustainable change involves maximizing the value of what you do and increasing your team's capabilities. All team members must embrace the tension between the two before change is effective, significant and sustainable. You cannot have one without the other.

Create Passion for Change:

Use every vehicle possible in communicating your vision and strategy for change. Maximize the value and benefits without hiding the temporary negatives and challenges.

Find a way to communicate the negative in a positive way. Great leaders communicate with words and deeds. Nothing undermines change more than leaders' behavior that is inconsistent with their words. Passionate leaders create passion through saturation communication.

Create a Persuasive Guiding Coalition:

Assemble a team of influencers outside the normal hierarchy strong enough to lead the change. They must have credibility, able to produce early wins, while laying the foundation for new systems, structures, and policies bringing significant and sustainable change.

Team members not committed to change; loyal to leadership's intent, and unable to persuade others to follow, should not be on this coalition.

Create a Clear Path to the New Vision

The guiding coalition empowers others to act by successfully communicating the new vision for change, giving them increased focus, and a new direction. Too often, team members get excited about change and want to help make it happen but an elephant appears to be blocking the path forward.

Sometimes the elephant is a mental block and sometimes the obstacle is real. Either way, great leaders find a way to remove it and allow creativity and innovation to flow unhindered.

Anchor Change in the Corporate Culture

Change sticks when it becomes a way of life and not just a new discipline everyone must follow. Only new behaviors produce significant and sustainable change. Until new behaviors become rooted in "that's how we do things around here" (shared values), they soon fall by the wayside.

Make a conscious effort by showing team members how these new methods; behaviors, and skills are making a difference. Everyone must make the connection or changes will not be sustainable.

Develop Leaders That Model & Support Change

Without supportive current and future leaders at every level, significant and sustainable change is doubtful. It only happens in organizations where teamwork, high commitment, and a constant learning curve is the norm.

Those in line for promotion to top leadership positions must personify the new corporate culture in their present position before consideration for advancement.

Lesson 42
Long-time leader's advice for new leaders

With every new leadership opportunity come new challenges. Success always provides more options than lack of success. Questions abound for new leaders, while the little voice inside says; "You have met your Waterloo this time."

In 1966, I began my leadership journey, made many mistakes over the years, but never quit. Take heart, the excitement of creating the future is what leadership is all about. As a life-long learner, I still have the privilege of working with leaders all over the world. Here are seven tips:

Have clarity about your Mission, Vision and Core Values.

All second and third generation organizations have a history, cultural priorities, a pecking order, and a, "This is how we do things around here," attitude. Study and get to know them well. Your leadership effectiveness begins there, not your idealistic vision for the future.

Reach out to all stakeholders

Some team members have been around a long time. Some may have even wanted your leadership position. Others have paid the price for the opportunity that is now yours. Never take for granted the sacrifices and emotions of those you now lead.

Start early building relationships as a servant-leader. Though you are first in line with authority and responsibility, be last in line for recognition and benefits. Make calls and seek council early and often. Learn the interests and hearts of those you lead. These relationships will serve you well for the long haul.

Put the best people in place

The "best" person may not always be the most skilled, but is the best fit for your team. Leadership is not about your production, but your ability to assemble a team of best people and teach them how to win. Ego-driven superstars are not looking for leadership and a team to join, but opportunities to show off their individual talent. Great leaders capitalize on diversity; a balanced mix of personalities, skill, and experience in people who know they are better as a team than any individual star.

Understand your public persona and external relationships

Never underestimate what the public and those who serve your organization think. In times of crisis or challenge, they are extremely important.

David Robinson |

Relationships built earlier determine just how important. Keep in mind, people you step on in your climb to the top, do not expect their outstretched hand on your fall from grace. Every leader disappoints at best and some fall. Relationships determine the length of the fall, and duration of the recovery.

Build productive networks inside and outside your organization

Not everyone who wants your attention should have it. Find creative ways to say no with kindness. One of the quickest ways to ineffectiveness and burnout is saying yes to everyone.

Do not be a loner. What you read, watch, and those you allow to speak into your life determines your leadership effectiveness. Choose healthy and productive leaders in other internal departments or similar organizations to form your network.

Do not fight the processes, systems, and demands

Instead, use them, and then improve them. Observe, listen and analyze before suggesting change. Leading change is fundamental to leadership, and the greatest challenge most leaders face, especially new ones.

Execute change slowly. Great leaders are always three to five years ahead of their stakeholders and one or two years ahead of their core leaders. The right decision made too early many times causes negative results. Know when to be among your team, ahead of them, and above them when making critical decisions.

Keep your eye on the ball named results

Leaders juggle many responsibilities; learn not to drop the one-called results. Activity, no matter how frenzied or passionate, never takes the place of results based on expected outcomes. Never accept a leadership role without knowing the expectations.

Unfulfilled expectations still bring life's greatest disappointments and most leadership failures. You can only hit a clearly defined target.

Lesson 43

Honor—What is it? Who deserves it? How do you give it?

King David's call for Mephibosheth to appear before him struck fear in Mephibosheth's heart because he was related to Saul, who tried to kill David on number of occasions. However, David did the unexpected and honored Mephibosheth, even having him sit at the King's banquet table.

David did this not because of who Mephibosheth was, but because of whom he represented. He was the son of Jonathan, whom David loved as his own soul. (See II Samuel 9.) We honor a person based on our perception of his importance or the importance of those he represents.

In this command, the Greek word for honor is timao. It means, *"To prize, i.e. fix a valuation upon; by implication to revere."* Reverence for others grows out of a proper fear of the Lord; since He is, the One Who created all men and established structures of authority. Therefore, true honor is based on our perception of the power, majesty, and holiness of God.

Reverence for God should cause us to honor every person as a representative of God, because He created them in His own image and has placed them in our lives for our benefit. On this basis, God instructs us to "honor all men. Love the brotherhood. Fear God. Honor the king" (I Peter 2:17).

Personal greed and pride destroy our ability to honor God or those who represent Him. In Mark 12, Jesus explains this truth in a parable about a wealthy master who sent one of his servants to a distant vineyard that he owned. The tenants who were caring for the vineyard beat the servant and drove him away rather than honoring him as the representative of the master and giving him the fruit of the land.

The master continued to send servants to the vineyard, but they experienced the same abusive disrespect. Finally, the master sent his beloved son, expecting the son would meet with respect. However, the wicked tenants said among themselves, "This is the heir; come, let us kill him, and the inheritance shall be ours" (Mark 12:7). Because of their failure to honor the authority that the servants and the son represented, the wicked tenants were put to death when the master returned.

We are not born with a natural tendency to honor God or others. We learn honor by learning to fear the Lord. Giving honor does not depend on the worthiness of the recipient; rather, it is a voluntary decision placing unconditional value upon a person because of who he is or whom he represents.

There is no question; our parents are a gift to us from God. Not only did God create them, they were chosen by God to bring us into the world and entrusted with the responsibility of training us in the fear and admonition of the Lord. Sometimes it is difficult to honor our parents because they make decisions that seem to be illogical. When this happens, we should ask ourselves, "What is God trying to tell us through them?"

Ask yourself, "If I were to view every person as a personal representative of God, how would my attitude and behavior toward him or her change?

Lesson 44
Honoring your spiritual leaders

There are three references to leaders in Hebrews 13. They are to be remembered (13:7); obeyed (13:17); and greeted (13:24). Faithful leadership in the local congregation must teach the Word of God with accuracy, passion, and inspiration. They must have a faith in that Word that is dependable and worth imitating and following. Spiritual leaders, who have oversight responsibilities in the Church, must recognize that their leadership is pastoral, accountable, and dependent.

Pastoral Leadership

(13:7) *"Keeping watch over your souls . . . "* Caring for sheep or sentry in the military. How are members to respond to diligent spiritual leaders?

Responsive obedience. Not blind, uninformed obedience, but thoughtful and caring. Otherwise the taught word has little impact or practically.

Respectful submission. If obedience applies to the leaders' teaching, then submission relates to the leaders' function. This clear recognition of authoritative leadership is essential to harmony in any group. Again, this does not advocate undiscerning or unintelligent submission.

Loving co-operation. If spiritual leaders have to labor under grim and hostile conditions, and rebellious followers—that never works out for members immediate or long-term good.

Accountable Leadership

Hebrews 13:7: *"As men who will have to give an account. Let them do this joyfully, and not sadly, for that would be of no advantage to you."*

This strongly conveys the future accountability of not only spiritual leaders but also members in the congregation.

One thing for certain, spiritual leaders in the end were not accountable to fellow members for their leaders' responsibilities. Every local Church leader should someone "over them in the Lord" to whom they are accountable.

Dependent Leadership

Hebrews 13:18-21: *"Pray for us; for we are confident that we have a good conscience, in all things seeing to live honorably. But I especially urge you to do this, that I may be restored to you the sooner. Now may the God of peace who brought up our Lord Jesus Christ from the dead, that great shepherd of the sheep, through the blood of the everlasting covenant, make you complete in every good work to do his will, working in you what is well pleasing in his sight, through Jesus Christ whom be glory forever and ever. Amen.*

In the exercise of local spiritual leadership's responsibility, the writer of Hebrews is depending on the prayers of the members, and both leaders and team members are dependent on the Great Shepherd for wisdom, guidance and ultimate victory.

Pray for your Leader and his team. Pray that they have a clear conscience and act honorably in all things. The leader's prayer for his team members is that the Lord equips them with everything good so they do His will, God working in them that, which is pleasing in His sight.

Equipped *with everything good* they will do that which honors him (*do His will*), which pleases Him (*that which is pleasing in His sight*) and which glorifies Him (*to whom be glory*).

Lesson 45
Leadership 101

Text: " . . . If God has given you leadership ability, take the responsibility seriously..." —Romans 12:8

Leadership = *"A person in a position of influence, responsible for the results of those under their direction."*

I. Four Levels of Leadership

1. Individual Leadership: *"Follow me as I follow Christ . . . "*—1 Corinthians 11:1

Marketplace, leading people closer to Christ or further away by the life you live there.
Church Family, leading people closer to the vision or further away by:

- Faithfulness and submission to the Pastor and his team. Hebrews 13:17: "Obey your spiritual leaders..."
- Faithfulness and submission to your Team Leader. Hebrews 13:17
- Faithfulness in paying your tithes and giving offerings. Luke 11:42 "these things ye ought to have done without neglecting the others..."

- Commitment to excellence in your service. Mark 7:37: "Jesus does all things well..."
- Commitment to share your faith. 2 Timothy 4:5: "Do the work of an evangelist..."
- Commitment to your Church's values. Acts 2:41-47 Core values

2. The Team Leader: (It's no longer about you—it's now about the TEAM)

Team leaders are strategic thinkers and goal setters. Team leaders develop other leaders and team building skills. Team leaders disciple them spiritually and empower them for their assignment. Find a leader who manages well, is a problem solver, and energized by fulfilling tasks.

Fill your team with those who have the gift of helps and a good balance of the other gifts that are passionate about the vision.

3. The Leader of Leaders: They have one or more team leaders reporting to them.
Requirements are the same as Team Leader has but do it for all Team Leaders.

4. The Organizational/Strategic Leader:
Determine direction for entire organization.
Disciple and train Leaders of Leaders.

II. Servant Leadership: *"For even the Son of man did not come to be ministered unto, but to minister and give His life for others."*

S—See the future and your personal connection to it without ignoring present reality.

E—Engage people—Follow a Paul, Mentor a Timothy and be a Barnabas.

R—Reinvent continuously—get better, more effective, and effective. Stay on a learning curve.

V—Value results—not just activity. Learn to set and meet goals.

A—Attitude determines altitude. Maintain a positive attitude and conversation.

N—Network with "Balcony People" and stay away from "Basement People."

T—Thrive on Acts 2 Basics: Prayer, Fellowship, Word, Giving, and Evangelism.

III. Follow The Leader (What the Pastor and his Team are trying to accomplish)

A. Balance meeting the shepherding and discipleship challenges through his "ministry management" team, while building a strategic leadership to help him create the future and fulfill the vision God has put in his heart.

B. He needs great leaders at all four levels committed to managing today better and optimizing every opportunity in creating a better future. Criticism and competition are out – cooperation and collaboration are in.

C. *You cannot be a great Leader if you are not a great **FAN**.* Seven Marks of a Great Fan:

- Come early—tailgate, fellowship and meet new friends.
- Stay late—love overtime and follow up with hurting friends.
- Never miss a game—season ticket holder, love the best seats close to the action.
- Memorize vital statistics—know all the players and performance.
- Is not weather sensitive—dress appropriately and start early.
- Pay the $$—never too high, work overtime, save up, and never try to sneak in.
- Are vocal—never have to guess whom they are rooting for.

IV. How it happens

Relational equity

1 Thessalonians 5:12: "Know them which labor among you and are over you in the Lord, and admonish you."

This is established through connection, collaboration, confidence, and competence.

Harmony

Psalms 133:2: *"How wonderful it is, how pleasant, when brothers live together in harmony! For harmony is as precious as the fragrant anointing oil that was poured over Aarons head, that ran down his beard and on to the border of his robe. Harmony is as refreshing as the dew from Mount Hermon that falls on the mountains of Zion. For there the Lord has pronounced His blessing forever more.*

How things flow together, what creates it?

- Aaron's head—authority, headship, and leadership.
- Beard—maturity, submission to God's Word, value wisdom of others, maintain a humble spirit.
- Border of the robe—influence, but not demanding or controlling.
- Dew from Mt. Hermon (Sion)—the mountain of revelation.
- Falls like rain on Mt. Zion—the mountain of praise.
-

Unity

Ephesians 4: 1-16: Uniting around the leadership team based on a common purpose (mission), vision (final frame), values (non-compromising principles), and goal-driven strategy.

Trust

- The mental and emotional glue that holds everything together and the lubricant that helps things flow together. How is trust built and maintained?
- Everyone's behavior must be mature, predictable, and consistent—no surprises.
- Communication and information must be clear, concise, and simple. Don't be cloudy, long-winded or complex.
- Keep your promises and commitments or let someone know in advance.
- Be candid and honest. Be emotionally mature—have adult comments, ideas, and opinions. Be able to receive before you start giving. Try to understand before wanting to be understood.

Lesson 46
Great leaders are emotionally healthy & spiritually

Mature Leadership is first a heart issue before it's a skill issue. You can't lead with integrity, influence and effectiveness if you are spiritually bankrupt and emotionally broken. Too often, we focus on performance when we need to look at maturity issues.

Leadership development too often looks at performance mechanics while giving token attention to internal challenges that determine longevity, success and significance.

If you combine all the information in the world with the most seasoned leadership skills, you will never make up for the lack of spiritual and emotional maturity. Of the Old Testament leaders who failed, most did so in the second part of their life. They didn't lack information or experience. They simply never grew up emotionally.

Leaders, who ignore their internal issues and rely on their resumes and high-powered interviews in gaining a place of leadership, do most of the damage in the Church and marketplace.

Empty and dysfunctional leaders never fill the lives of their followers with significant opportunities for personal and organizational growth. Leaders are not great because they have outstanding talent and skill. They are great because they are emotionally healthy and spiritually mature. They have grown and matured internally in their walk with God as they pursue a constant learning curve for skill, knowledge and healthy values.

Who a person is must be more important than what a person does. If you don't think so, ask the employees of Enron, Tyco, Global Crossing and Arthur Anderson. Immature leaders drove these and other major corporations to collapse and failure. Their leaders were gifted and skilled but, without a moral compass and emotional maturity. You learn great skills through significant learning opportunities over time.

Spiritual leadership maturity and competency is developed similarly but must be accompanied by other factors.

A good friend Steven Sisler says great leadership begins with knowing who you are and who you are not. The family culture you were born into and the values instilled during your maturing process, determines *who* you are. What, you carry out of that experience into adulthood, has a lot to do with your spiritual and emotional maturity.

If your experience was positive, you have a foundation on which to build and improve. If the experience was negative, you must not ignore the realities that came with that less-than-ideal experience. Using God's infinite grace and mercy, is how you lay a new foundation. It's never too late or too early to develop healthy emotions and spiritually mature habits and values.

The space between what makes you tick and what ticks you off is developed early in life. Many factors constantly challenge and modify this reality beyond your childhood and teenage years. Those factors include early work place experiences; education beyond high school; your sense of destiny or God given call; your circle of friends or lack of significant relationships; how you handle conflict (internal and external) and a host of other issues that impact the development of your life story.

Great leaders, understand, accept and embrace who, they are and their own personal life story. They find their own voice for expressing it and make no apologies for which they are and are not.

This does not mean they no longer try improving, but efforts to improve are built on a foundation of emotional health and spiritual maturity in a culture of honesty. They no longer kid themselves or try to impress others with who they are or cover up who they are not.

Only leaders God has developed to this point are in a position to lead other effectively. Spiritual and emotional maturity must not be for your personal benefit, but for the greater benefit of those who God allows to touch your life. You, your life and your leadership may touch a few or many. The number is not as important as the testimony of those who do. How do they feel about themselves and their future as they walk away from you?

May those who touch your life and experience your leadership be encouraged and better because of your spiritual and emotional maturity.

Lesson 47
Great leaders inspire & empower

One of the great success stories is the Post-it® Note invented by Art Fry. He didn't invent the adhesive or the paper on which it was used. But, he put the two together. His inspiration for the Post-it® Note came back in the 1970s when he sang in his church choir and used scraps of paper to mark selected pages in the hymnal. He recalls thinking about needing a paper bookmark that would stay put but easily removed without damaging the hymnal.

Around the same time Art's colleague, Dr. Spencer Silver, was doing research on adhesives. He would come up with a low-tack adhesive that stuck lightly to many surfaces, yet remained sticky even after you repositioned it. Art soon realized his friend's discovery was the answer to his problem. He applied some to the edge of a piece of paper and now had a removable and reusable bookmark that would not fall out.

Realizing his invention's full potential, he brought the idea to 3M's management who provided him with a research team. Eighteen months later, they were showing samples to the marketing department, and as is often said, *the rest is history!*

What's not so widely known is that Art Fry's discovery was not entirely a fluke. It was the natural outcome of a 3M policy that encourages scientists like

Art Fry to spend up to 15% of their time working on projects they personally believe in. Without the time and support to pursue his sticky.

Bookmark, Art Fry's idea might have just remained an idea—not a finished product. Millions of dollars of the *Post-it* brand products are sold every year worldwide. Other breakthrough products came on board such as Scotch © tape.

One of the common complaints I hear from team members is that their leader does too much micromanaging. Most senior leaders do not mean to and most of the time, don't realize they are suffering from *looking over your shoulder disease*! It was obvious Art Fry was not micro-managed.

Wise leaders know that talented, gifted and motivated team members do their best work when given space to be creative and innovative in fulfilling their assignment. If you have the right person to begin with, they shouldn't be expected to justify every decision but only the expected result.

Leadership is not about control, motivation and certainly not manipulation. It is about influence, empowerment, and inspiration. Too many times, for a variety of reasons, we take the first available person rather than the best available person. Too often decisions made in haste and momentary urgency come back to bite you. There is one thing worse than having a vacancy on your team. It is having the wrong person in that position. Now instead of just having one problem, you have two.

If you are sure, you have the right person for the team, and then teach them what they need to know; train them so they can perform competently; then coach them to excellence. After you have done that, aim them in the right direction; hold them accountable for the agreed upon results; get out of their way and become their biggest cheerleader. This works at all levels of leadership.

Why don't more leaders do this?

First, they fear losing control. Control is a management function—not a leadership issue. You can lead your church or marketplace effort or you can manage it. But, you cannot do both with any degree of success for long.

Second, most inexperienced or untaught leaders do not understand how micromanaging can be so counterproductive. Isn't it odd you never hear about micro leading?

Third, they don't understand the benefits of adequate teaching, training and coaching. If they do understand the value they lack the patience, perseverance and necessary time to complete the process, and the results are the same.

Fourth, they probably did not get the right person for the opening on their team. As I often say, "Be slow to appoint so you won't have to dis-appoint."

Fifth, many times there is not clarity on the mission, vision, values and strategy. Without clarity on these four pillars of any organized effort, the best team members will struggle, become frustrated and eventually leave you.

The one key ingredient in all of this is trust. The glue holds every team together, especially through the tough times and the long haul. It takes significant time to earn trust, and lost in a moment. My experience tells me, if you have the right person; compete steps one through five; continue building relational equity; and give team members room, they will likely share and promote your vision. Because, *your* vision is now *our* vision.

Remember, the measure of your success is how creative, innovative and passionate your team is without you!

Lesson 48
How great leaders serve their generation

"David, after he served his own generation by the will of God . . . " —Acts 13:36.

Can one person change the course of history? Is it possible for one person to have impact on the world? Every person decides, whether his or her footprints will last beyond their lifetime or disappear into the sands of time.

You may not change the course of world events, as did Joseph, Daniel, the Apostle Paul, D.L. Moody, Billy Graham and many others. Only God determines that. But, all of us have the opportunity to change the *history* of those who touch our lives and experience our leadership during our generation.

Leadership is all about the future. A leader is one in whom the future is seen in support of the present and in spite of the past. History has given us many great examples to follow.

However, in the later part of the 20th Century, something went wrong with our understanding of leadership, both in the church and the public arena. The same decades that brought so much fresh understanding and revelation in the revival of leadership after World War II also brought us some of the worst scandals our world has ever seen in the corporate and church worlds. Enron, World Com,

Adelphia, Tyco, Global Crossing and Arthur Anderson became household words as they filled our TV screens for months.

This lack of moral courage and integrity brought disgrace to the highest office of our land and culminated in a President who will be known for many things, not the least of which will be, "It depends on what the meaning of is - is." I believe this declaration by the *leader* of the free world set the stage for the flood of immorality and corruption gripping our nation today.

The Church has not escaped this dramatic decline and has suffered greatly as well. Once, mighty men of God fell from high profile ministries to utter disgrace and humiliation because they lacked integrity, moral fortitude, and most of all, a daily walk with God to go with their God-given leadership skills. That was a fall, from which the Church has still not fully recovered. She longs for 21st Century leadership that seeks for Godly significance before success in the eyes of men.

God calls everyone for a particular mission and destiny, not just a select group. Some of the *called* are *called out* to lead while others are called to manage. Leaders are summoned to a place of leadership when the cause for which they were born arises in their generation. This was the case in I Samuel 17 when David was summoned to the battlefield at a very critical time, and leadership in Israel was lacking.

At times elected leaders will find themselves following a summoned leader whose time has come i.e., David vs. Saul. Great leaders hear the challenge (Goliath) and respond while others hear the same challenge and hide in the palace.

Whether you are an elected leader, an appointed leader, or even recognized as a leader, you are summoned by God to make a difference in the lives of people of your generation because the life of Christ flows through you.

Leaders serve their generation in many different ways.

Here are three: First, we can be *"a brook in the way."* Psalms 110:7 says, *"He (Jesus) shall drink of the brook in the way; therefore shall he lift up the head."* This could very well refer to the brook Kidron that Jesus drank from on his way to the Garden of Gethsemane to pray before going to the cross. As leaders, we all need a "brook in the way" to refresh us when we get weary and we all need to be a "brook in the way" for others.

Second, we can be a rock to help stop the drift in the lives of people. *"And a man shall be as an hiding place from the wind, and a covert from the tempest; as rivers of water in a dry place, as the shadow of a great rock in a weary land."* Isaiah 32:2 Many of those we lead today are weary. The sands of their lives are shifting every day. We can make a difference by being a rock that helps slow the drift in their ever-changing landscape called life.

Third, we can be a voice of hope in a world that seems hopeless to know what to do. *"I (Jesus) have many things to say...he that sent me is true...and I speak to the world those things which I have heard of him"* (John 8:26).

Before we can be a voice of hope, we must have a heart that hears. As leaders, we must learn to love the sound of our own voice in praise and worship, and then use that voice to teach others how to sing. Someone once said, *"Give me shoes and they last a year, give me a song of hope and it lasts a lifetime."* That is leadership serving their generation well.

God has summoned you, your leadership matters, so go change the course of someone's life today.

Lesson 49
Five agreements that produce strong teams

Releasing informed, inspired, trained, and empowered servant-leaders at every place of ministry opportunity is the church able to fulfill the *Great Commission* and the mission and vision of every local church and marketplace ministry.

Committed, engaged, and anointed servant-leadership is the key ingredient fostering a spirit of revival and creating the atmosphere in which spiritual growth takes place.

Good interpersonal relationships are vital but the most important component in building powerful and effective teams understands and total commitment to a *clear common purpose*.

The GOAL of all ministry teams is not merely getting along (spirit of agreement), but alignment around the *clear common purpose*. In a spirit of cooperation and allegiance to the values, are desired results realized.

The power of teamwork (spirit of agreement) flows out of alignment between the interests and commitment levels of individual team members and the mission (clear—common purpose) of that team. To achieve such agreement, alignment, attunement and allegiance, every team member must see our mission, vision, and values as:

CLEAR—I SEE IT!

Every team member must understand the teams purpose—not just his or her own individual task.

Without this understanding, agreement, alignment, attunement, and allegiance is lacking. Do not assume this understanding exists. Team leaders and members keep communicating until the *light goes on.*

RELEVANT—I WANT IT!

The Mission must be relevant and make sense to all team members - not just the leader. Every team member must find value in his or her contribution to the mission. *"How does what I do help us win"* must be answered.

WORTH IT—I WILL PAY THE PRICE!

All team members must believe the mission (clear - common purpose) has significant value and is worth their effort and sacrifice to achieve.

The Disciples died for the mission Jesus gave them. What mission is your team willing to live or die?

URGENT—I WANT IT NOW!

Leaders must have a bias toward action with results. There is a clear time-value attached to the achievement of our mission. There are other valuable activities and pursuits outside the agreed upon mission, but at some point, the mission must take priority.

Without a sense of urgency by all team members, the best strategy, the most ambitious goals, become just another *good idea.*

ACHIEVEABLE—I BELIEVE IT IS POSSIBLE!

You must believe our mission is achievable and persuade the team! You must learn the art of goal setting. Jesus said, *"Go into all the world."*

Your mission (clear - common purpose) must be big enough to challenge and inspire, and achievable with God's help.

Team Commitments

I understand the mission and vision with no questions.

I agree with it and support it wholeheartedly.

I am committed to make it my third priority (After God and family) or drop from the Team.

I am clear about my part and responsibility to our mission. Great leadership is not about getting the work done through people, but *getting people done through the mission!*

Lesson 50
How to set goals & realize your life's potential

Twenty Questions to Help You Define Your Goals

1. If you were to living your life to its fullest what is the first change you have to make?

2. What areas of your life could or should be upgraded or tweaked?

3. What could we work on now that would make the biggest difference to your life?

4. How would you feel about doubling that goal?

5. What are you tolerating/putting up with that needs to change?

6. What do you want more of in your life? (Make a list)

7. What do you want less of in your life? (Make a list)

8. What are the three things you are doing regularly that do not serve you or support your life goals and ministry vision?

9. How can you make your goals more specific?

10. What would be the biggest impact from achieving your goal(s)?

11. What would you attempt now if resources were no object and you knew you would not fail?

12. How can we make this something we are moving toward, rather than trying to move away from?

13. What do you love?

14. What do you dislike?

15. What is the one thing you would love to do before you die?

16. Is now the right time to make a commitment to achieve these goals? If not, when?

17. What could we work on immediately that would put a smile on your face?

18. For your life to be fulfilled, what would have to change?

19. What do you really, really want?

20. What is the one change you could make to your lifestyle that would give you more peace and satisfaction?

Goal Setting Basics

How do you hit a *target* you cannot see?

Have you set a date?
Have you defined, what you need to know, relationships you must develop, resources you must generate, etc.?
Have you created a strategy with solid goals?

Why some people don't set goals

Lack of direction; not time, money, people.
Confuse activity with achievement. Goals must be specific and meaningful.
Depression, usually does not affect those who have specific short-term and life goals. Logic will not help, only actions.

F.E.A.R. is the #1 reason the 97% do not set goals. (**F**)alse (**E**)vidence (**A**)ppearing (**R**)eal

Risk. There is always a risk in setting goals that you may not reach them. But, you are better off than not setting them at all. You don' accidentally accomplish anything of value by accident. Choices dictate everything.
Lifetime goals should dictate daily goals. What did you do today that brought you closer to your lifetime goals? People who do not set goals and reach them consistently always work or serve those who do.

That is why the 3% who do not set goals work or serve the 97% who do.

You will always have an excuse why you do not. If you wait, (on whatever) you will never set goals. Goal setting is about decisions and commitments before it becomes a process and a way of leading.

Pay Attention to your goals

1. You need multiple goals to be balanced.
2. You need big goals to stretch your capacity in every area of life.

"All I have is this little bitty frying pan"
—Colonel **Sanders, KFC**

You must work on your goals every day.

3. Make a commitment – put some pressure on yourself.
4. Be careful with whom you share your dreams and goal.
5. Your words define your future and fulfill your goals. Only by meeting your goals do you create a better tomorrow for yourself, those you love and those who touch your life.

Training Fleas: "Do we walk or take a dog today?" Put a lid on their jar and eventually they won't hit the lid anymore. Remove the lid and they won't fly away either. People are the same way! You are conditioned either by positive or by negative people. Motivation always comes from within. Setting goals helps you build a winning attitude.

Seven Types of Goals

1. Wisdom (dependent on gaining more knowledge and using it wisely)
2. Stature (physical & divine health through discipline)
3. Spiritual (favor with God through Discipleship)
4. Socially (favor with man through emotional maturity)
5. Calling (in the Church or the Marketplace)
6. Family (the 1st Church through responsibility and relationship)
7. Financial (ability to give beyond your own needs)

Seven Steps in Setting Goals

1. Write it down.
2. Set a firm deadline.
3. Identify the obstacles and speed bumps
4. Contacts, groups, and individuals you must meet or work with.
5. What do you need know or learn i.e., skills, information, etc.
6. Make a plan of action.

7. Why do you want to reach it? What are the benefits?

Setting Goals is Biblical

The Father set goals

"Before the earth was formed the lamb was slain" He sent his son on a clear and compelling mission. Scripture gives the Church a clear assignment.

Ephesians 4 gives clear assignments to Church and Marketplace ministers.

Jesus set goals

1. "For the prize that was set before him . . . "
2. "I have come to destroy the works of the enemy..."
3. "My hour has come . . . "

All those that God used set goals

1. Adam & Eve; "Be fruitful, multiply and cover the earth.
2. Noah; "build me an ark...go forth and replenish the earth . . . "
3. Abraham; inherit the Promised Land.
4. Moses; "go set my people free"
5. Joshua; "conquer and dominate the Promised Land"

6. The New Testament Church goals: "Go into all the world and preach the Gospel," "Baptize all believers," "Make disciples of all nations," "Equip the saints for the work of the ministry so they can:

a. Cast out devils
b. Heal the sick and afflicted
c. Set loose them that are bound
d. Set the captives free
7. Lord's commitments to the Church – for those who align with His goals.
- Send the Holy Spirit to comfort and guide.
- The right to use His Name.
- Signs of using my name would follow you everywhere.
- I will never leave you (go ahead) or forsake you (leave you behind).
- When it is all over, I will come and get you.
- You will reign with me forever.

About the author

Since 1966, Dr. David Robinson has developed his leadership and management skills through a wide range of opportunities and challenges. He has a Bachelors Degree in Applied Theology from Logos Christian College & Seminary in St. Augustine, Florida. He has a Masters Degree in Organizational Leadership from Southern Seminary in Augusta, Georgia and a PhD from Aidan University in Jacksonville, Florida.

Dr. Robinson is an adjunct Professor for Logos University and Aidan University. He also serves as the Chair of their Clergy/Market Place Ministry coaching and consulting department and represents Logos nationally and internationally.

David can be contacted through:
coaching4ministers.com

32100894R00154

Made in the USA
Charleston, SC
09 August 2014